Entrepreneurship

Entrepreneurship

ALAN L. CARSRUD AND
MALIN E. BRÄNNBACK

GREENWOOD GUIDES TO BUSINESS AND ECONOMICS
Wesley B. Truitt, Series Editor

GREENWOOD PRESS
WESTPORT, CONNECTICUT • LONDON

Library of Congress Cataloging-in-Publication Data

Carsrud, Alan L.
   Entrepreneurship / Alan L. Carsrud and Malin E. Brännback.
      p. cm. — (Greenwood guides to business and economics, ISSN 1559–2367)
   Includes bibliographical references and index.
   ISBN 0–313–33689–X (alk. paper)
   1. Entrepreneurship.   I. Brännback, Malin E.   II. Title.
   HB615.C295 2007
   658.4′21—dc22   2006038687

British Library Cataloguing in Publication Data is available.

Library of Congress Catalog Card Number: 2006038687
ISBN-13: 978–0–313–33689–8
ISBN-10: 0–313–33689–X
ISSN: 1559–2367

First published in 2007

Greenwood Press, 88 Post Road West, Westport, CT 06881
An imprint of Greenwood Publishing Group, Inc.
www.greenwood.com

Printed in the United States of America

The paper used in this book complies with the
Permanent Paper Standard issued by the National
Information Standards Organization (Z39.48–1984).

10   9   8   7   6   5   4   3   2   1

This book is dedicated to entrepreneurs
throughout the world and to those who have allowed us
to write about the entrepreneurial experience: Patrik, Anton, Anna,
and Axel Rantanen and Danny Babineaux, Alex, Jeff, and Clara Lee Harrell

Contents

Illustrations

Series Foreword

Scanning the pages of the newspaper on any given day, you'll find headlines like these:

"OPEC Points to Supply Chains as Cause of Price Hikes"
"Business Groups Warn of Danger of Takeover Proposals"
"U.S. Durable Goods Orders Jump 3.3%"
"Dollar Hits Two-Year High Versus Yen"
"Credibility of WTO at Stake in Trade Talks"
"U.S. GDP Growth Slows While Fed Fears Inflation Growth"

If this seems gibberish to you, then you are in good company. To most people, the language of economics is mysterious, intimidating, impenetrable. But with economic forces profoundly influencing our daily lives, being familiar with the ideas and principles of business and economics is vital to our welfare. From fluctuating interest rates to rising gasoline prices to corporate misconduct to the vicissitudes of the stock market to the rippling effects of protests and strikes overseas or natural disasters closer to home, "the economy" is not an abstraction. As Robert Duvall, president and CEO of the National Council on Economic Education, has forcefully argued, "Young people in our country need to know that economic education is not an option. Economic literacy is a vital skill, just as vital as reading literacy."[1] Understanding economics is a skill that will help you interpret current events that are playing out on a global scale, or in your checkbook, ultimately helping you make wiser choices about how you manage your financial resources—today and tomorrow.

It is the goal of this series, Greenwood Guides to Business and Economics, to promote economic literacy and improve economic decision-making. All seven books in the series are written for the general reader, high school and college student, or the business manager, entrepreneur, or graduate student in business and economics looking for a handy refresher. They have been written by experts in their respective fields for nonexpert readers. The approach throughout is at a "basic" level to maximize understanding and demystify how our business-driven economy really works.

Each book in the series is an essential guide to the topic of that volume, providing an introduction to its respective subject area. The series as a whole constitutes a library of information, up-to-date data, definitions of terms, and resources, covering all aspects of economic activity. Volumes feature such elements as timelines, glossaries, and examples and illustrations that bring the concepts to life and present them in historical and cultural context.

The selection of the seven titles and their authors has been the work of an Editorial Advisory Board, whose members are the following: Alan Carsrud, Florida International University; Alan Reynolds, Cato Institute; Wesley Truitt, Anderson School of Management at UCLA; Walter E. Williams, George Mason University; and Charles Wolf Jr., RAND Corporation.

As series editor, I served as chairman of the Editorial Advisory Board and want to express my appreciation to each of these distinguished individuals for their dedicated service in helping to bring this important series to reality.

The seven volumes in the series are as follows:

- *The Corporation* by Wesley B. Truitt, Anderson School of Management at UCLA
- *Entrepreneurship* by Alan L. Carsrud, Florida International University, and Malin Brännback, Åbo Akademi University
- *Globalization* by Donald J. Boudreaux, George Mason University
- *Income and Wealth* by Alan Reynolds, The Cato Institute
- *Money* by Mark F. Dobeck and Euel Elliott, University of Texas at Dallas
- *The National Economy* by Bradley A. Hansen, University of Mary Washington
- *The Stock Market* by Rik W. Hafer, Southern Illinois University-Edwardsville, and Scott E. Hein, Texas Tech University

Special thanks to our senior editor at Greenwood, Nick Philipson, for conceiving the idea of the series and for sponsoring it within Greenwood Press.

The overriding purpose of each of these books and the series as a whole is, as Walter Williams so aptly put it, to "push back the frontiers of ignorance."

Wesley B. Truitt, Series Editor

NOTE

1. Quoted in Gary H. Stern, "Do We Know Enough about Economics?" *The Region,* Federal Reserve Bank of Minneapolis (December 1998).

Preface

Entrepreneurs and the firms they create are the engines of economic growth and wealth creation. The names of entrepreneurs, past and present, are known worldwide, be they Henry Ford or Bill Gates. This volume is based not only on the rapidly growing empirical knowledge about entrepreneurs and the entrepreneurial process, but also on the authors' extensive work with entrepreneurial firms around the world in a wide variety of industries. These entrepreneurial firms, most of which are small and medium-sized enterprises (SMEs), are responsible for 75 percent of all new jobs created.[1] Government officials and policy makers worldwide have begun to see it as highly important to promote entrepreneurship. But, even transnational organizations see entrepreneurship as the forerunner of prosperity and development. For example, in December 2000 the European Union (EU) adopted the five-year Multiannual Programme for Enterprise and Entrepreneurship. This program focused on new economy challenges to SMEs. This was the result of the Lisbon European Council in 2000, where the EU chose a new strategic objective for the coming decade: to become the most competitive and dynamic knowledge-based economy in the world. Entrepreneurship had taken the center of the economic stage, and entrepreneurs and innovators were perceived as the leading actors. However, entrepreneurs are often seen as miracle workers, or the silver bullets of modern times, by governmental leaders as when President George W. Bush called upon the American entrepreneurial spirit to rebuild the damaged New Orleans after Hurricane Katrina and to rebuild New York following 9/11.

While entrepreneurs and small business owners may not be able to work miracles, they form the overwhelming majority of businesses if measured by number. Small firms dominate every nation in the world, including China and India. According to the US Small Business Administration in 2002, there were 22.9 million businesses in the United States and 99.7 percent of these were classified as small firms.[2] While most small firms tend to remain small, an important percentage (3 to 10 percent) manages to grow beyond 100 employees. However, the definition of what is a small firm or an entrepreneurial firm varies by country.

In the United States a firm is considered small if it is independently owned, operated, and financed; has fewer than 100 employees; and has relatively little dominance of its industry. Two-thirds of US firms employ less than five persons and 78 percent of the firms employ less than ten persons. For comparison, within the EU member states a firm is considered small when any two of the following requirements are met: (1) the turnover (sales) is less than €6.25 million, (2) the balance is below €3.125 million, or (3) there are less than fifty employees in the firm. Correspondingly, a firm is classified as large when any two of the following criteria are met: (1) the turnover exceeds €40 million, (2) the balance is at least €27 million, or (3) there are more than 250 employees.

Small firms are interesting not just because they are so many, but also because they create new jobs and usually employ the vast majority of a country's working population. As small firms are responsible for 75 percent of all new jobs created, government officials and policy makers see it as highly important to promote entrepreneurship. In fact, there has never been a more favorable time for creating new firms in many countries. However, despite strong backing from governments, entrepreneurial activity in many Western countries remains low. The Global Entrepreneurship Monitor (GEM) has annually analyzed entrepreneurial activity in some thirty-five to forty-two countries worldwide since 2000. The GEM measures total entrepreneurial activity (TEA), which measures the number of persons aged between eighteen and sixty-four who are considering starting a firm. Although globally there are millions of people considering starting a firm, the proportion of the population in most Western economies is not high at all. While the United States is considered the leader in entrepreneurship, only 12.4 percent of the US population in 2005 was thinking of starting a venture (Table P.1).

TABLE P.1
Total Entrepreneurial Activity

Country	2000	2001	2002	2003	2004	2005
Finland	8.1	7.7	4.6	6.9	4.4	5.0
United States	16.6	11.6	10.5	11.9	11.3	12.4

Note: This table has been compiled using data from the annual GEM reports from 2000-2005. In GEM 2005 the TEA measure has been changed into early-stage entrepreneurial activity, which includes nascent entrepreneurial activity and new business ownership. This new measure corresponds to the TEA measure used in previous reports.

In Finland, the home country of the mobile phone giant Nokia, entrepreneurial potential was just 5 percent (total population 5.2 million), which
is 2.5 times lower than in the United States. This is a striking paradox,
because Finland was rated by the World Economic Forum for the fourth
consecutive year as the most competitive nation and the fourth most innovative country in the world. In Sweden, the third most innovative country
in the world, entrepreneurial activity was even lower, 4 percent. Finland
shows the second highest expenditure on R&D, measured as a percentage of
GDP, after Sweden. In 2004 the level was 3.5 percent.[3] That is, the trend in
entrepreneurial activity is downward despite increased efforts to create a
trend in innovation. While entrepreneurship and innovation are related,
they are clearly not the same thing. Innovations do not necessarily create the
entrepreneurs to take those to the market. Researchers will continue to
measure entrepreneurship on a national level, which will tell us something
about the entrepreneurial climate in various countries, but that is beyond
the scope of this volume.

We think that a much more fruitful approach is to look at individual
entrepreneurs and firms regardless of national boundaries. Nearly everyone
in the developed world recognizes Wedgwood, Heinz, Estee Lauder,
Microsoft, Dell Computers, Apple, and Ford Motors as successful brands.
These companies were founded by entrepreneurs and many are still run as
family firms. These companies were at one time small but have prospered,
some of them for centuries, even when their competitors failed.[4] These firms
and the entrepreneurs behind them have inspired a lot of other entrepreneurs. These entrepreneurs have become role models for many, and it is
indeed insightful and educating to read about their lives. What do we know
about them? What factors influenced the birth and early development of
these later day economic giants? While these are interesting questions, they
are not as important as *How do entrepreneurs identify opportunity and address
the personal and social risk associated with the starting of a new venture? Is it like
the title of the best-selling book by Sahar and Bobby Hashemi: Anyone Can Do
It: Building Coffee Republic from Our Kitchen Table?*[5] How is it done? Is there
a general road map, like a cookbook, that can take you from the "IDEA" to
"IPO"?

This volume is for a wide spectrum of readers, including students and
teachers of entrepreneurship, but more specifically for budding entrepreneurs,
would-be small business owners, and innovators who are exploring the possibility of starting their own venture (both for profit and not-for-profit). This
book tries to answer the question "How do I do it and where do I start?" It is
said that over 75 percent of Americans want to be their own boss, but we
know that less than 20 percent of them undertake the steps in the journey.

Hopefully, this book will help those undecided to take their first steps down that road, and those already into their journey avoid some of the pitfalls and perils along the way. Even if after reading this book some decide that entrepreneurship is not for them, at least they now have an appreciation of perhaps the single most important economic activity in the world.

This book focuses on what it takes to be "entrepreneurial," because these attitudes and behaviors are relevant to over 460 million people worldwide every year who are engaged in the early stages of starting an enterprise. While economies of the world depend upon job and wealth creation through entrepreneurship, personal wealth creation by many is shunned because they fear taking the first steps toward being an entrepreneur. They hesitate because they do not know if they have the skills to succeed. On the other hand, there are those who believe they know it all and lose everything because they did not acknowledge some of the obvious pitfalls in starting any new venture. We hope this book will help both of these groups of potential entrepreneurs. These are the critical lessons that we hope every entrepreneur will know even when everything they have been taught formally in school has been forgotten. While this book is based on both empirical research and theory on entrepreneurship, it is tempered by the authors' personal experiences gained while helping to start numerous companies in industries from biotechnology and airlines to restaurants and cleaning services in many different countries.

CHAPTERS

CHAPTER 1: WHAT IS ENTREPRENEURSHIP AND IS IT RIGHT FOR YOU?

This chapter offers various perspectives on entrepreneurship. It describes the importance of entrepreneurship and the pursuit of opportunity in greater detail. It also describes entrepreneurial minds, types, and personalities, so that readers who may be considering starting a firm can identify the entrepreneur in themselves. The goal is to help the reader understand what will be demanded of them if they choose entrepreneurship as a career alternative.

CHAPTER 2: ENTREPRENEURS AND THEIR WORLD

This chapter explains how important it is for an entrepreneur to understand the business environment they enter when launching a new venture. It shows that the concept of a business environment is indeed complex and, above all, constantly changing. Change occurs not only because of the entrepreneur's actions but also because business is in a constant flux. Entrepreneurs operate in networks, and these networks evolve constantly. Networks are important to entrepreneurs both as networks of contacts and as networks of information. Critical is a discussion of how entrepreneurs use networks to both develop their ideas and advance their new ventures. Suggestions for successful network development are given.

CHAPTER 3: IDEA GENERATION AND CREATING THE CONCEPT STATEMENT

In this chapter the authors consider the very core of entrepreneurship. That is, how do some people identify opportunities and others do not? How are the opportunities evaluated, and how are concepts developed for exploiting those opportunities? This chapter provides some idea-generation exercises and methods for rapid screening of opportunities for potential new ventures. The key is to exploit the best opportunities that fit specific goals, desires, and passions. Critical to this chapter is to get the reader to begin to write down their business concept and start on an executive summary for their business plan. The reader is also asked to develop a five-minute "elevator-pitch" as an exercise.

CHAPTER 4: ENTREPRENEURIAL STRATEGIES: DEFY COMPETITION AND ENTER THE MARKET

For many starting entrepreneurs the task of handling competitors is new and many are quite unprepared for the challenge. This chapter deals with how the entrepreneur can deal with competition through different forms of innovations, be it product innovation, process innovation, or business concept innovation. Furthermore, this chapter covers different forms of collaboration that an entrepreneur may take advantage of in entering a market, including strategic alliances, partnering, acquisition, or franchise.

CHAPTER 5: CREATING NEW PRODUCTS AND SERVICES

This chapter carefully underlines the importance of addressing customer needs, wants, and fears in developing products and services. It describes the criteria that successful products and services have to meet to gain customer acceptance, including financial consideration with respect to new products and services. A review of a stage-gate model of product development is provided.

CHAPTER 6: BUILDING A STRATEGY: UNDERSTAND THE INDUSTRY AND COMPETITION

Here the authors provide a brief overview of the concept of strategy and describe the role of strategy in entrepreneurial companies. Key issues of managing the industry environment are discussed as well as the business environment at large, including the global business environment and legal environment. As intellectual property forms an important part of a business strategy and the way a firm may compete, these issues are also covered in this chapter.

CHAPTER 7: THE MARKET AND CUSTOMER GROUPS

This chapter focuses on how markets and customers can be identified, categorized, and reached based on a variety of criteria. However, all activities are based on understanding and responding to customer wants, needs, and fears. The chapter also describes different ways to segment the market.

CHAPTER 8: DEVELOPING INTERNAL PROCESSES—OPERATIONS, PRICING, AND FINANCE

Once the external world has been examined, it is then critical for the entrepreneur to look at the proposed internal operations of their venture to see what they need to exploit the opportunity they have identified earlier. This chapter describes the importance of an operations plan, pricing strategies, as well as financial needs and resources that the entrepreneur may have and be able to address.

CHAPTER 9: MANAGEMENT AND HUMAN CAPITAL

People make a new venture work or fail. They are the biggest resource (and expense) any entrepreneur has. In this chapter there are discussions of management of the new venture and the differences between being a manager and an entrepreneurial management team. Specific attention is paid to hiring, out-sourcing personnel, compensation, employee management, and motivation. The roles of advisors and boards are discussed along with how to find critical support from networks.

CHAPTER 10: GROWTH AND ENTREPRENEURIAL FAMILY FIRMS

This chapter moves beyond the issues of opportunity recognition and planning and into the fundamentals of initiating a business. This section focuses on the issues of growth, such as how to manage growing organizations, building effective entrepreneurial management teams, and the management of change. This chapter also addresses how to keep the entrepreneurial spirit alive in a larger organization. Finally, this chapter covers a special topic of entrepreneurship, family owned and managed firms.

APPENDIX: PUTTING A PLAN TOGETHER AND
AVOIDING PITFALLS

This appendix provides an overview of the dos and don'ts in writing and presenting an effective business plan. It pulls concepts from the previous chapters and asks the reader to create an executive summary of a business plan. In addition, an example of such a summary is provided. The focus of this chapter is how to craft a compelling story as the basis for their business plan.

NOTES

1. Erkko Autio, GEM 2005 High Expectation-Entrepreneurship Summary Report, www.gemconsortium.org; Paul D. Reynolds and Sammis B. White, *The Entrepreneurial Process: Economic Growth, Men, Women, and Minorities* (Westport, CT: Quorum Books, 1997); Howard E. Aldrich, *Organizations Evolving* (London: Sage Publications, 1999).

2. For more precise information please consult http://www.sba.gov/aboutsba/sbastats.html; http://www.sba.gov/size/part121sects.html.

3. WEF, www.wef.org; European Innovation Scoreboard, 2005; Statistics Finland, 2005.

4. Nancy F. Koehn, *Brand New* (Boston: Harvard Business School Press, 2001); Paul Freiberger and Michael Swaine, *Fire in the Valley: The Making of the Personal Computer,* 2nd ed. (New York: McGraw-Hill, 2000).

5. Sahar and Bobby Hashemi, *Anyone Can Do It: Building Coffee Republic from Our Kitchen Table* (Chichester: Capstone, 2002).

PART I

ENTREPRENEURSHIP AND YOU

One

What Is Entrepreneurship and
Is It Right for You?

Who is an entrepreneur, or what is entrepreneurial, are questions considered among the most difficult part of studying entrepreneurship.[1] In 1988 William Gartner published an article, considered a classic in the field, titled "'Who Is an Entrepreneur?' Is the Wrong Question," which challenged the assumption that there is a stereotype of the entrepreneur.[2] However, the question persists despite the claim that it is the wrong question and despite many researchers reaching the same conclusion as Gartner. Neither researchers nor practitioners have quit searching for an entrepreneur.[3] In this book we also deal with what researchers have for more than three decades attempted to create—a commonly accepted definition of entrepreneurship. While they have not succeeded in this attempt, it is important to understand why. The issue has been addressed from *what* happens when an entrepreneur acts, *why* they act and *how* they act, and then *who* this actor is, as if there was a specific *homo entrepreneuricus* who is equipped with certain characteristics.[4] The rationale follows a line of reasoning that assumes that "it" can be engineered, provided we first know what "it" is, or provided we can first generate the list of characteristics to look for in an individual and then find such persons; the rest is really an education issue.

Despite Gartner's claim that *who* is the wrong question, this way of asking haunts us and often makes would-be entrepreneurs wonder if they have what "it" takes. For example, we are frequently confronted with doubting colleagues who question whether entrepreneurship can be taught; whether entrepreneurs are really born and whether there really is a gene that needs to be identified. Gartner continues to point out that asking *why* tends to get answered with *who*; "Why did X start a venture? Because X has certain inner quality or qualities."[5] So, we look for role models to learn from them.

It sometimes also looks as if we really want to create a system that would effectively generate new entrepreneurs who look alike.

In this chapter we present you with our understanding of what entrepreneurship is, which is based on research findings as well as our personal experiences. Our perspective acknowledges that there are certain personality types and motivational styles that appear to be common to successful entrepreneurs, although some claim that there are no typical personality traits among entrepreneurs.[6] However, we do want to emphasize that these personality types and motivational styles are often the same kinds as those that drive any ambitious person, whether it is someone who wants to be a successful airline pilot, dentist, any professional per se, or even a sports star. Achievement motivation may be general, but the entrepreneurial view of that motivation may be what is unique. We describe what we call an entrepreneur's cognitive mind map that distinguishes them from what we call ordinary managers (who may be successful as well). Recent research has found differences in the cognitive style of entrepreneurs.[7] We challenge the widespread perception (or even myth) that entrepreneurs are extreme risk-takers and that they are born rather than made through learning or experience. In other words, we claim that some skills can be taught and some characteristics are attitudes that can be influenced through education, but some, that are not teachable in the same way, are clearly closer to "art."[8]

We argue that any intelligent person with an achievement and goal orientation is capable of being *entrepreneurial*. But being entrepreneurial need not result in the actual creation of a firm. In its widest meaning, entrepreneurial can mean getting things done. This definition has its origin in the Swedish (not French) language—*företagsam*. As one of the authors speaks Swedish as her native tongue, this explanation, while surprising, is perhaps more understandable. This brief linguistic tour is motivated also because many claim that the term "entrepreneur" was coined by the French Jean-Baptiste Say in the early nineteenth century,[9] and others will argue it was another Frenchman, Richard Cantillon.[10]

The linguistic comment is appropriate, as the word "entrepreneurship" translates into many other languages in ways that provide a much wider, or at least differing, meaning than the English meaning. In Finnish, the word for entrepreneur is *yrittäjä*, which translates as someone who *tries*. The Swedish word is *entrepreneur* and is often associated with an undertaker or a builder—one putting an end to some activity and the other creating the new, often on the initiative of somebody else.[11] This word has a very narrow meaning. A much wider meaning is provided by the word *företagsam*, which literally means *to be a doer, to get a thing done*. The word breathes action and activity as opposed to apathy and inaction. It is the action and activity that will be our guiding star throughout this book.

We start with showing the importance of entrepreneurship for economic activity, not just in the United States but also in the Nordic countries and other parts of the world. Even the People's Republic of Vietnam has its *Danh Tu's* (entrepreneurs). We will argue: if there is an entrepreneur there is active life, there is motion, there is GO. Supporting entrepreneurship is critical to the economic health of regions and nations. Entrepreneurship is the source of sustainable economic prosperity for nations, societies, regions, corporations, small firms, and individuals. Entrepreneurship is as important in Ecuador, Peru, Poland, Finland, Spain as well as the United States.

In this chapter we describe what drives individuals to become entrepreneurs, and events in the environment that often trigger entrepreneurial behaviors. The goal is to help anyone who contemplates starting a firm to understand what will be demanded of the person—oneself—if entrepreneurship is chosen as a career alternative or the choice of lifestyle.

WHY IS ENTREPRENEURSHIP IMPORTANT?

One thing researchers and practitioners have been able to agree upon is that entrepreneurship is important for the economic prosperity of individuals, regions, and nations. According to the US Small Business Administration in 2002, there were 22.9 million businesses in the United States and 99.7 percent were classified as small firms. For comparison, by the end of 2004 there were 232,305 companies in Finland (a country with 5.1 million people), with 99.8 percent classified as small. Although the criteria for what is considered *small* slightly vary in the United States and Finland, small firms are important to both nations. In both nations small firms have been responsible for 75 percent to 80 percent of all new jobs created, whereas large firms—those known in the United States as Fortune 500—have been job destructors, that is, they employ fewer total employees than they did ten years ago, a trend that has been going on for the past twenty years. What may seem less obvious is that small firms are more efficient in many other important ways than their larger counterparts. In the United States, on an average, small firms produce thirteen to fourteen more patents per employee than do large firms, and small firms are able to respond more quickly and operate more efficiently.[12]

While new firms create jobs they also contribute to the economic development of regions. The initial success of Silicon Valley and Route 128 in the mid-1970s propelled these areas into worldwide admiration. Although both areas experienced a slowdown, from which Route 128 did not manage to recuperate until much later, they are to this date commonly regarded as role models for similar regional and national initiatives worldwide. These initiatives are on a national level, referred to as "innovation systems," with a primary aim to increase entrepreneurship through massive support of innovative activity such as technology development and R&D. It is assumed that this in turn is the same as supporting entrepreneurship. Research has shown the usefulness of national innovation systems (NIS) for institutions devoted to innovation[13] on a macro level, but for the single entrepreneur an innovation system remains abstract and not terribly useful.[14]

Thus, entrepreneurship is important to economic wealth creation at the national and individual levels. Data reveals that most firms are small. In fact, most firms are small when they start and only 3 percent grow beyond 100 persons,[15] and most never add any employees at all. It is important to understand that many entrepreneurs actually do not want to hire employees, preferring often to outsource all but the most critical aspects of their operations. That is, national interests to create growing firms may be contradictory to personal desires.

As individual citizens it is important to understand that entrepreneurship significantly impacts our own lives and those of our fellow citizens as a vital source of new job creation and a source of a vast majority of new technology and products. Entrepreneurship also plays a key role in providing effective and innovative solutions to environmental and social problems. In many countries, particularly in the United States, many cultural institutions, universities, and others have received considerable donations from successful entrepreneurs who have contributed to the prosperity of their nation, community, or even globally. Examples are Bill Gates, who has been said to donate over 90 percent of his personal fortune to his foundation to address world health issues, and Ted Turner, who has given over a billion dollars to the United Nations. Many universities and foundations in the United States carry the names of successful entrepreneurs, for example, the Ford Foundation and the libraries built by Andrew Carnegie of US Steel. As a majority of firms are small, this has led to entrepreneurship often being associated with small firms. However, it is important to stress that even corporations can be entrepreneurial; in fact, enabling sustained innovativeness and competitiveness require firms to be entrepreneurial. This has been called corporate entrepreneurship.[16] In this book our primary focus is nevertheless on small firms although entrepreneurial behaviors can occur even in not-for-profits.

The fact that entrepreneurship is such an embedded phenomenon in our society can partially explain why people wanting to become entrepreneurs may have such diverse reasons for their decision. For many, it is surely personal wealth creation, that is, a dream to one day become very rich; for others, it may be the only existing way to earn a living or feed the family. For some, it can be a desire to change one's life and even the world. For example, a growing area within entrepreneurship is social entrepreneurship, which often takes the form of not-for-profit. For policymakers and other bystanders the reasons may once again be very different from those already mentioned. However, it is important to understand that entrepreneurship is not a magic wand or a silver bullet. Anyone who becomes an entrepreneur is embarking on a road full of "to dos." Entrepreneurship is about doing and making, it has to be lived. Knowing what to do will not automatically result in a successful firm. One has to constantly make the venture successful.

WHAT IS ENTREPRENEURSHIP?

Cantillon defined the economic role of the entrepreneur as one bearing the risk of buying at certain prices and selling at uncertain prices. Say added factors of production into the definition, and the entrepreneur became a protagonist or a *hero* of economic activity in general,[17] a notion that also corresponds nicely with the Swedish word *företagsam*.

For many, the father of modern entrepreneurship is the Austrian born Joseph A. Schumpeter, who published his book *The Theory of Economic Development* in 1934.[18] The core of Schumpeter's definition of entrepreneurship is *innovation*. Entrepreneurs are those who carry out new combinations.[19] Following this view, entrepreneurship is defined as *purposeful innovation*. This definition tells us that innovations can take at least five different forms:

- A new good or a new quality of a good
- A new method of production not previously tested, that does not need to be founded upon scientific discovery
- Opening of a new market, that is, a market that a firm has not previously entered, whether or not this market has existed before
- A new source of supply of raw materials, irrespective of whether this source already exists or has to be created first
- The carrying out of new organization

We think it is necessary to go beyond innovation when defining entrepreneurship. Therefore, we add William Baumol's description of an entrepreneur— an individual who exercises what in the business literature is called *leadership*.[20] In fact, Baumol claims in his 1968 article that managers do not exercise leadership! Another description that is useful here is the one by Al Shapero.[21] He described entrepreneurial behavior as the kind of behavior that includes (1) taking initiative, (2) organizing or reorganising of social and economic mechanisms to turn resources and situations to practical account,

and (3) the acceptance of risk and failure. A major resource used by the entrepreneur is himself or herself

Finally, we need to acknowledge Kirzner's view on entrepreneurship. While
Schumpeter's entrepreneur is an innovator, Kirzner's entrepreneur is, according to the neo-Austrian perspective,[22] an actor in the process-conscious market theory who exhibits deliberate behaviors. That is, where Schumpeter's
innovator is shifting the costs and revenue curves (through innovation), Kirzner's
entrepreneur is, through entrepreneurial alertness, able to notice that *the
curves have shifted*. According to Kirzner, sources of entrepreneurship are to be
found in information or knowledge *asymmetry*. The entrepreneur possesses
unique knowledge, which enables him or her to extract economic rent from
market ignorance. For some odd reason Kirzner's and Schumpeter's views have
been considered as opposite poles, that is, entrepreneurship will take either
form. Scott Shane summarizes differences between Schumpeterian and
Kirznerian entrepreneurship in a way that presents each characteristic as the
other's opposite,[23] which at first glance seems acceptable, but to our understanding, perhaps too simplified (Table 1.1). We argue that Schumpeter and
Kirzner most likely are opposite sides of the same coin.

We have in Table 1.1 shaded the perceptions that we find problematic. First
of all, we disagree with Shane's argument that Kirzner's entrepreneur is not
based on new knowledge. Kirzner argues that entrepreneurship is based on the
entrepreneur's ability (alertness, which is based on the knowledge he but
nobody else possesses) to identify market ignorance with respect to a certain
opportunity.[24] This helps him to spot an opportunity. Once the opportunity
is pursued by the entrepreneur and the market becomes aware, the opportunity certainly arrives as a new piece of knowledge to the market and all the
other would-be entrepreneurs. A different kind of a *Eureka!* phenomena.

Kirzner's entrepreneur, who can be described as being market oriented, may
well have been doing careful market analysis and, with his knowledge of existing innovations and an ability to combine these innovations, is able to identify

TABLE 1.1
Schumpeterian versus Kirznerian Opportunity Recognition

Schumpeterian Opportunities	Kirznerian Opportunities
Disequilibrating	Equilibrating
Requires new knowledge	Does not require new knowledge
Very innovative	Less innovative
Rare	Common
Involves creation	Limited discovery

Source: Scott Shane, *A General Theory of Entrepreneurship* (Cheltenham: Edgar Elgar, 2003), p. 21.

a viable opportunity. His ability to combine must certainly be regarded as the ability to generate new knowledge, in a very Schumpeterian way. This combination can be very innovative and is certainly very creative. But whether the discovery is limited or not depends on the economic effects created over time. For example, the Internet in 1969 was certainly based on new knowledge, it was very innovative and unique, and involved creation. But the number of people who saw a benefit (or even knew about it) of it at the time was very limited—limited to highly skilled computer scientists and certain university personnel.

The World Wide Web, again unique, innovative, and involving creation, was at first a rather limited discovery in terms of for whom it provided a benefit. It was the combination of these two and the front end, again new knowledge and indeed innovative and creative, that made the whole bundle very common. Those who possessed information technology knowledge saw an ocean of opportunities, which the ignorant market did not. We saw the dot-com era, which once changed the market knowledge and caused the market to equilibrate, and around the turn of the twenty-first century turned into a deflated bubble. Many firms ceased to exist, because the market had reached its carrying capacity.

This short passage in our history may lead some to think that entrepreneurs are shameless scoundrels, and some may have been so, too. The important thing to realize here is that the economy in most countries was catalyzed by entrepreneurs. When considering the importance of the entrepreneurial function to the development of a nation's economy, such considerations are often made with respect to Schumpeter's perspective on entrepreneurship. The issue is important from both a research and a practice perspective and shows no sign of decline, with more than 200 regional innovation systems studies published between 1987 and 2002 and new papers published monthly.[25] As we have pointed out, entrepreneurship is not just about small companies, but most often they are small businesses.

Entrepreneurship, however, is not only about starting firms. Entrepreneurship and entrepreneurial firms can be very mature in age and they can be extremely large as well. Examples of established large firms that can be described as entrepreneurial are 3M, Nokia, Heinz, and Starbucks.[26] In the so-called street-talk, one occasionally hears the idea that entrepreneurs are unscrupulous promoters who make money at the expense of others. However, one must realize that many firms carry the names of their founders and few founders want their name or the name of their firms to be associated with bad publicity. There is not a single firm that has been able to create success based on bad publicity.

If we argue that entrepreneurship contributes to economic improvement, entrepreneurship exists in both small and large firms. Growth, innovation, and flexibility are characteristics often found in entrepreneurial firms. Many entrepreneurs have a desire for independence, and entrepreneurship can be driven by altruistic ambitions rather than personal ones. Thus, we can arrive at a definition that we find most appropriate, with perhaps the exception of necessity entrepreneurship, that is, when entrepreneurship is the only way to earn a living. This definition allows for a coexistence of Schumpeter's and Kirzner's perspective as if opposite sides of the same coin. We define entrepreneurship as *the process by which individuals*—either on their own or inside organizations—pursue opportunities without regard to the resources they currently control. [Emphasis added by authors][27]

We view entrepreneurship as an attitude toward management, but perhaps even more as an attitude toward life as much as it is about starting and running a firm. We recognize that some firms do not seek growth, although our views are that growth is a natural goal for anyone seeking sustainable economic development. Now to the question of how does one see opportunities to pursue?

THE PURSUIT OF OPPORTUNITY

Why do some persons leave well-paying jobs to become entrepreneurs or undertake a change to a lifestyle entrepreneur such as starting a winery or an art gallery rather than working for a large firm with big benefits? Stevenson and Jarillo define opportunity as being a "future situation deemed desirable and feasible."[28] Accordingly, the answer to the question would be, they got fed up and wanted to realize, for example, a dream of starting a winery. The well-paying job has rendered the dream feasible.

Earlier in the chapter we said that Schumpeter's entrepreneur creates opportunities through innovation, whereas Kirzner's entrepreneur sees opportunities because he or she possesses unique information or knowledge. Kirzner's entrepreneur seeks to capitalize on market ignorance, whereas Schumpeter's entrepreneur creates new markets. Hence pursuing an opportunity can go along either path. However, pursuing opportunities is about showing a willingness to make commitment and acceptance of change and uncertainty. Perceptions of one's desires and capabilities vary and may be quite loosely connected to reality. It is, however, this willingness that drives the future entrepreneur to pursue opportunities beyond resources that one controls or owns.

As we may recall, entrepreneurship is about seeking new combinations and this very much involves combining resources that other people possess. This is a feature typical to the knowledge-based society we live in today. As Drucker has described a century ago, a craftsman could learn the skills he needed for the rest of his career during the few years as an apprentice.[29] Today, any successful professional has to take the path of lifelong learning to constantly renew his knowledge base, or he will be rendered obsolete. Not only do scientific advances occur at such a pace that it is impossible to stay abreast, but new knowledge is also created constantly and it is impossible for any human to store that amount of knowledge. Therefore, we have to combine sources of knowledge. Thus, personal networks and relationships have become a source for entrepreneurial opportunities. Earlier firms aimed at owning sources of production. Owning was the same as control. Today, cooperation and collaboration can provide a mutually beneficiary control mechanism over resources and thus enable the pursuit of an opportunity.

It has been shown that opportunity recognition and entrepreneurial intentions are closely connected.[30] That is, a person finding an opportunity desirable and feasible is likely to create a venture. Ajzen's theory of planned behavior[31] and Shapero's model of the entrepreneurial event[32] have shown convincingly that action is dependent on intentions and that intentions are driven by personally perceived desirability and feasibility. Absent intentions, no action occurs.

Concept development will be discussed more extensively later in this book. At this point it is sufficient to conclude that concept development occurs once the opportunity has been considered feasible enough and desirable to warrant further attention. There are basically three ways to recognize an opportunity:

1. an active and systematic search of the external environment
2. fortuitous discovery
3. it is the creation of the entrepreneur.

A heuristic model for opportunity recognition is shown in Figure 1.1. At this point, it is what involves the prevision stage that is interesting. As we can see, it contains a number of factors. Many are not only rooted in prior personal experience, but also anchored in the environment. Some of these factors can be actively and systematically surveyed and even controlled; others are less controllable, such as environmental forces. An alert individual may be able to envision a future activity, perceive it as personally desirable and feasible. This is said to trigger a *Eureka!*, which is also called having an *Idea*.

But merely having an idea is not enough. It has to be a good one that will really grow into a business. Whether the idea is that good will be known only after it has been tested. But to minimize a complete walk in darkness and an unpleasant surprise, it is possible to evaluate the idea and carefully consider its worthiness before a final decision to create a venture is taken. Nevertheless, it is not necessary to bring about radical changes to create a venture.[33]

Research has shown that alertness is a moderating factor of opportunity recognition, that is, necessary but not sufficient alone. Entrepreneurs with advanced educational degrees tend to do less systematic search as they have

FIGURE 1.1
Heuristic Model for Opportunity Recognition

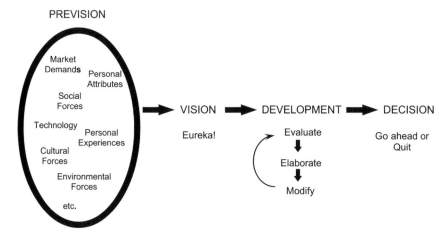

Source: Connie Marie Gaglio, *The Entrepreneurial Opportunity Identification Process.* Doctoral Dissertation (University of Chicago, Chicago, 1996).

experience and prior knowledge—and perhaps stronger self-confidence—which will lead them to a more focused search.[34] For some, opportunity recognition is a multistage process; for others, it is a single-stage process. Opportunity recognition can be market-driven, recognizing market ignorance as Kirzner notes, or product- and technology-driven, as seen by Schumpeter.

Since every entrepreneurial endeavor occurs in unique social contexts, it is important to understand that people will perceive opportunities very differently. Someone who works in a scientific research laboratory in a major urban research university will see very different opportunities from someone living on a farm in the Midwest, Finland, or in the outback of Australia. Even if one sees an opportunity with far-reaching implications, it may not be acted upon because it was not perceived as desirable or feasible. We would strongly underline the need for contextualizing entrepreneurship. In certain environments and contexts, some *Eurekas* may be bigger than others. *Eureka* is not necessarily a universal phenomenon.

ENTREPRENEURIAL MINDS

Not too long ago it was possible to get a bank loan without a business plan, and many small firms operated (and still do) based on the mind map of the founding entrepreneur. They had no strategy and no budget. All that was necessary to know existed underneath the balding skull of the aging entrepreneur. But the entrepreneur may not be either old or balding and we may laugh at this. But, as recently as spring 2006, one of the authors interviewed a number of technology entrepreneurs, including one employing ten persons. The entrepreneur had a hunch that more money was going out than coming in. When the author asked to see the latest budget the entrepreneur replied that he had never done a budget in his life! The entrepreneur was actually quite happy but thought he might have a problem at his hands. This is not the story of somebody on the brink of losing his mind, but in fact a very common description of entrepreneurial reality and in a way a very intuitive description of an entrepreneurial mind.

One way to really understand entrepreneurs is to examine how they think. This involves studying the cognitive maps or schema that they employ when developing their concepts, creating a viable business model, or formulating their marketing and sales strategies. We use the term "cognitive maps" to refer to mental prototypes of what the concept or business is—a template. Some entrepreneurs may have been very systematic in the process of starting a firm; others may not have thought too much but just acted on pure intuition. The latter has certainly been the rationale for our above described entrepreneur.

We know, for example, that serial entrepreneurs have more clearly defined mental prototypes, and richer prototypes than new entrepreneurs, because they have prior experience to rely on. Repeat entrepreneurs show greater business acumen as their cognitive maps also include possible business and revenue models. We may do the same observation on persons who have worked in larger firms and then decided to start their own firm. They, too, may have a map of a business, a vision of what they want to do. Even those entrepreneurs who have failed have an ability to see the reality differently. We know from prior research that education alone is not sufficient to develop an ability to purposefully coordinate actions as an entrepreneur. There is no substitute for experience, as it appears to significantly impact perceptions of what critical success factors or combination of factors may lead to positive results.

We do not say that only experienced persons can become successful entrepreneurs. However, it would be naïve to think that experience does not matter. Successful entrepreneurs have learned to meld a wide variety of inputs from the perceptions of others such as mentors, networks of advisors, advisory boards, and others. These individuals possess a variety of experience and the cognitive maps, which a naïve person lacks and an inexperienced person does not know how to combine in a purposeful way. Therefore, observing others can be instrumental in entrepreneurship.

Different kinds of industry or product experience produce different kinds of strategic decision-making frameworks for future use. General industry experience and/or experience in developing technology do not necessarily translate directly into specific product differentiation strategies. For example, technology experience may not generalize across specific technology-based products, which may explain why a manager with technology experience from one industry may not be able to utilize that experience in another related industry with different products, let alone entirely different unrelated industries. Research suggests that management skills in a large firm may not transfer perfectly to the different orientations of being an entrepreneur. This means that a manager may lack the entrepreneurial experience needed to successfully start up and grow a venture despite product or industry experience.

Many think that a small firm is just a downsized large company. But that is not the case. Especially, if the company is starting, there are hardly any assets, there are hardly any routines and even fewer people. The people in the organization may be competent, but the company has not created its core competences yet, which are embedded, deeply rooted in organizational values, cultures, and action. A manager may have experience from operating in such an environment, but none in building such qualities in a new one. For example, simply providing would-be technology entrepreneurs with general management education will not give them the kind of perspectives needed to perceive industry and opportunities very differently from experienced managers. This book thus focuses on using practical knowledge and intelligence (and education) to achieve success in life.

THE ENTREPRENEURIAL PERSONALITY

Are there any particular personalities typical to entrepreneurs?[35] A colleague who has for more than twenty-five years studied and worked with entrepreneurs, and is one himself, described entrepreneurs in the following way:

I can say they are "*innovative*" but not necessarily inventors. They are "*creative*" but the canvas on which they draw is a "*firm*" or "*organization*." Entrepreneurs have a *sense of excellence*: they think they are special and unique and are not just satisfied with the mundane. But it is also clear that there are no virtues without vices, and entrepreneurs have egos, sometimes very big ones. It would be hard for me to see a highly successful entrepreneur walk around saying to all he passes, "I am sorry for being successful."

As already discussed, one key characteristic of an entrepreneur is a strong motivation for personal achievement—apart from being capable of recognizing an opportunity. This is reflected in the quote above. Interestingly, while we know that organizations in the process of recruiting new employees go through lengthy and expensive selection procedures often involving external consultants and psychological tests, we rarely hear anyone undertaking similar measures on entrepreneurs. In fact, human resources are one of the most critical resources in small firms, so one might assume that some formal selection method might be called for. However, consulting textbooks on entrepreneurship reveal a different picture. Human resources can be a subtitle under a chapter with a different title, or a separate chapter. It is, however, among the last chapters in the books—hidden in the back. Normally, nothing is said about how to find a suitable entrepreneur, a little more is said about how an entrepreneur should find skilled entrepreneurial employees. Basically, this is not seen as an important issue. The interesting thing is that most books on human resource management ignore the human resource issues facing start-up firms and seem to assume that this function is the same as in larger firms.

Research on entrepreneurial personalities and entrepreneurs' ways of behavior has revealed certain characteristics commonly found in successful entrepreneurs (Figure 1.2). These are (1) cooperativeness and a strong team player, (2) strong desire to work hard, (3) strong desire to learn new and different things, (4) ability to listen to others and network, (5) not competitive, but visionary and goal setting, (6) strong self-efficacy, (7) coach or a trainer, and (8) not any more risk-prone than other professionals.

What is interesting is that these are the same characteristics that make any professional successful, be they doctors, lawyers, academicians, or airline pilots. These qualities are typical in an achievement-oriented personality, and a key quality there is *cooperation*. An entrepreneur is someone who holds and exhibits entrepreneurial attitudes and a strong belief in oneself and one's unique ability, which we also sometimes describe as *ego*.

FIGURE 1.2
Strong Entrepreneurial Personal Characteristics and Behavior

We also know that entrepreneurs appear to have a stronger capacity to perceive, express, transform, or discern forms and see unseen patterns. Entrepreneurs are frequently expected to see things others do not or see events in the environment that impact opportunity recognition. Entrepreneurs need good communication skills, which will enable them to use words effectively. It is needed for writing effective business plans and speaking effectively, such as to persuade financers to invest.

Finally, most of us have observed that entrepreneurs tend to have a "fire in the belly," a "passion," which keeps them going when everyone else would have given in and quit. This passion is visible when entrepreneurs refer to their venture as their "baby." We also know that entrepreneurs tend to be overly optimistic about their abilities, which in a way can be seen as passion. Passion can here be a major motivator, but in a negative sense it makes the entrepreneur persist with an opportunity that is no longer viable. It is necessary for an entrepreneur to be able to walk away and have sufficient resources and energy to try again with another idea another day. The baby metaphor is instrumental here as it explains why entrepreneurs have such difficulty in letting go, in admitting that an idea was not good enough. A colleague explained passion in the following way:

I am frequently asked by students with several ideas to help them decide which one they ought to go after . . . I really never listen to the words they speak. I listen to the way they speak and the tone of their voices. You can tell immediately when they start talking about something for which they have passion.

ENTREPRENEURIAL TYPES

Charles Handy authored a book titled *Gods of Management*, in which four Greek gods were ascribed certain managerial types that acted as change agents; that is, the book was on the changing work in organizations.[36] Other similar ways of categorization of organizations or strategists have been presented of the years, sometimes described as schools of thought.[37] Handy's book was both entertaining and insightful for those familiar with Greek mythology. However, what purposes this kind of categorization serves other than pedagogic ones can be debated. We have, for exactly pedagogic reasons, chosen to describe entrepreneurial types that we have over the years observed to exist. In other words, this categorization is based on our observations, not statistically proven empirical studies.

We maintain that there are primarily four types of entrepreneurs, although one of them is a managing entrepreneur. The first is the achievement entrepreneur, who is typically associated with being high in the need to achieve. These individuals are frequently portrayed as having tremendous energy and a propensity to take charge. They are never ones to let something just happen but in fact take initiative. As they are often leaders with a strong sense of personal responsibility, they have a strong commitment to their organization and believe they control their own lives. These individuals, because they believe they can do almost anything, wear many hats in their ventures and try to be good at lots of things. While these may seem to be the characteristics of the ideal entrepreneur, the person may not always be really good at everything and not always the best team player. This is critical as evidence over the years show that fast-growing firms require fast-growing entrepreneurial teams.

The second is the salesman entrepreneur, who uses people skills and the "soft side of management." These individuals are exemplified as possessing feelings for other people's needs and wants. They typically use the soft-sales approach when pushing their venture and actually prefer spending time selling and letting someone else manage the business. While this may seem a hands-off entrepreneur it is actually a critical style when one is trying to develop products or services customers want and need, and is certainly critical if the firm's success requires marketing and sales expertise, as in retailing, hospitality, or service-based industrial sectors.

The third can be seen as the stereotype of the technology entrepreneur, that is, the idea developer. These individuals often invent new products or services, new niches, or develop new processes for existing products. As individuals they are drawn to the world of ideas. Most likely, because of their analytic intelligence, these individuals take calculated risks. However, they can be frequently idealistic. Analytic intelligence allows them to think their way through situations. This works as long as there is not a "bear chasing you."

These three are facing the fourth, the manager, who likes and tries to take charge. This type is highly competitive and is not always the most cooperative or a team player. They are usually positively disposed to those with authority, such as a board of directors or external investors. They seem to genuinely enjoy power and prefer larger organizations to entrepreneurial firms. These individuals are frequently effective marketers, but not always great personal sales people. When they do sell they use logic and persuasion to sell. Their real strength is in managing the existing firm. In other words, they possess qualities that are often defined as management skills.

SUMMARY

What is "entrepreneurial" remains difficult for many to define. To this date one of the most difficult issues in the field of entrepreneurship is to establish who or what is an entrepreneur.[38] To most ordinary persons and practicing entrepreneurs this seems purely an academic problem as most of us know someone who is an entrepreneur. However, it is important to understand that there are multiple definitions of who is an entrepreneur and what is entrepreneurial. This indicates that there is as much "art" in this topic as there is "science."

CONSIDER THIS

Think of entrepreneurs whom you know personally and ask the following questions:

- What kinds of skills, knowledge, contacts, and resources have they brought to bear on their venture?
- Did they see changing patterns as they formed in the marketplace?
- How did they prepare their plan? (Many might say they did not write a formal plan, but ask them if they had a strategy and a plan in their mind that they followed and updated as they went along.)
- How did they take action on the opportunity they saw, or did they just talk about it?
- Did they have to revise, retrench, and recommit in the process of making their venture possible?
- How did they consider the challenge?
- Did they consider the frustration and the possibility of failure?
- What qualities do they have?

NOTES

1. Mark Casson, *The Entrepreneur: An Economic Theory* (Totowa, NJ: Barnes & Noble, 1982).

2. William B. Gartner, "'Who Is an Entrepreneur?' Is the Wrong Question," *American Journal of Small Business* 12 (1988): 11–32.

3. Scott Shane and Sankaran Venkataraman, "The Promise of Entrepreneurship as a Field of Research," *Academy of Management Review* 25 (2000): 217–226.

4. Howard H. Stevenson and J. Carlos Jarillo, "A Paradigm of Entrepreneurship: Entrepreneurial Management," *Strategic Management Journal* 11 (1990): 17–27.

5. Gartner, "Who Is an Entrepreneur?"

6. Ibid.; Peter F. Drucker, *Innovation and Entrepreneurship* (New York: Harper Business, 1985).

7. Albert Bandura, "Social Cognitive Theory: An Agentic Perspective," *Annual Review of Psychology* 52 (2001): 1–26.

8. Colette Henry, Frances Hill, and Claire Leitch, "Entrepreneurship Education and Training: Can Entrepreneurship be Taught? Part I," *Education and Training* 47 (2005): 98–111; Henry, Hill, and Leitch, "Entrepreneurship Education and Training: Can Entrepreneurship be Taught? Part II," 158–169.

9. Drucker, *Innovation and Entrepreneurship*; Gartner, "Who Is an Entrepreneur?"

10. Stevenson and Jarillo, "A Paradigm of Entrepreneurship."

11. Bengt Johannisson, *Entreprenörskapets väsen* (In Swedish: The Essence of Entrepreneurship) (Lund: Studentlitteratur, 2005).

12. http://www.sba.gov/aboutsba/sbastats.html; see statistics Finland, www.research.fi or www.yrittajat.fi; Autio, Erkko. 2005 GEM 2005 High Expectation-Entrepreneurship Summary Report. www.gemconsortium.org; C. E. Bamford and G. D. Bruton, *Small Business Management, a Framework for Success Instructor's Edition* (United States: Thomson, 2006).

13. Phil Cooke, "Regional Assymetric Knowledge Capabilities and Open Innovation. Exploring 'Globalisation 2'—A New Model of Industry Organisation," *Research Policy* 34 (2005): 1128–1149; Chris Freeman, "Continental, National and Sub-national Innovation Systems—Complementarity and Economic Growth," *Research Policy* 31 (2002): 191–211; Richard R. Nelson, "National Innovation Systems: A Retrospective on a Study," *Industrial and Corporate Change* 1 (1992): 347–374; Annalee Saxenian, *Regional Advantage: Culture and Competition in Silicon Valley and Route* 128 (Cambridge: Harvard University Press, 1994).

14. Joseph W. Duncan and Douglas P. Handler, "The Misunderstood Role of Small Business," *Business Economics* 29 (1994): 1–6.

15. Howard E. Aldrich, *Organizations Evolving* (London: Sage Publications, 1999); Howard E. Aldrich and M. A. Martinez, "Many Are Called, but Few Are Chosen: An Evolutionary Perspective for the Study of Entrepreneurship," *Entrepreneurship Theory & Practice* 24 (2001): 41–56; Paul D. Reynolds and Sammis B. White, *The Entrepreneurial Process: Economic Growth, Men, Women, and Minorities* (Westport, CT: Quorum Books, 1997); Stevenson and Jarillo, "A Paradigm of Entrepreneurship."

16. Drucker, *Innovation and Entrepreneurship*; Gartner, "Who Is an Entrepreneur?"

17. Stevenson and Jarillo, "A Paradigm of Entrepreneurship."

18. Joseph A. Schumpeter, *The Theory of Economic Development* (Oxford: Oxford University Press, 1934).

19. William J. Baumol, "Entrepreneurship: Productive, Unproductive and Destructive," *Journal of Business Venturing* 11 (1990): 3–22; Drucker, *Innovation and Entrepreneurship*; Gartner, "Who Is an Entrepreneur?"; Schumpeter, *The Theory of Economic Development*; Stevenson and Jarillo, "A Paradigm of Entrepreneurship."

20. William J. Baumol, "Entrepreneurship in Economic Theory," *American Economic Review* 58 (1968): 64–71.

21. Albert Shapero, "Social Dimensions of Entrepreneurship," in *The Encyclopedia of Entrepreneurship*, eds. Calvin A. Kent, Donald L. Sexton, and Karl H. Vesper (Englewood Cliffs, NJ: Prentice Hall, 1982), 72–90.

22. Dan Hjalmarsson and Anders W. Johansson, "Public Advisory Services—Theory and Practice," *Entrepreneurship & Regional Development* 15 (2003): 83–98; Israel M. Kirzner, *Competition and Entrepreneurship* (Chicago: University of Chicago Press, 1973); Kirzner, *Perception, Opportunity, and Profit* (Chicago: University of Chicago Press, 1979).

23. Scott Shane, *A General Theory of Entrepreneurship* (Cheltenham: Edgar Elgar, 2003).

24. Kirzner, *Competition and Entrepreneurship*; Kirzner, *Perception, Opportunity, and Profit*.

25. Cooke, "Regional Assymetric Knowledge. Exploring 'Globalisation 2.'"

26. Nancy F. Koehn, *Brand New* (Boston, MA: Harvard Business School Press, 2001).

27. Stevenson and Jarillo, "A Paradigm of Entrepreneurship."

28. Ibid., 23.

29. Peter F. Drucker, "The New Society of Organizations," *Harvard Business Review* 70 (1992): 95–105.

30. Barbra Bird, "Implementing Entrepreneurial Ideas: The Case for Intentions," *Academy of Management Review* 13 (1988): 442–454.

31. Icek Ajzen, "Attitudes, Traits and Actions: Dispositional Prediction of Behaviour in Social Psychology," *Advances in Experimental Social Psychology* 20 (1987): 1–63.

32. Bandura, "Social Cognitive Theory"; Norris F. Krueger, "The Cognitive Infrastructure of Opportunity Emergence," *Entrepreneurship Theory & Practice* 24 (2000): 5–23; Norris F. Krueger, Michael D. Reilly, and Alan L. Carsrud, "Competing Models of Entrepreneurial Intention," *Journal of Business Venturing* 15 (2000): 411–432; Schumpeter, *The Theory of Economic Development*; Shapero, "Social Dimensions of Entrepreneurship."

33. Mike Sutton and Chris West, *The Beermat Entrepreneur* (London: Pearson Prentice Hall Business, 2002).

34. Lynne G. Zucker, Michael R. Darby, and Jeff S. Armstrong, "Commercializing Knowledge: University Science, Knowledge Capture, and Firm Performance in Biotechnology," *Management Science* 48 (2002): 138–153; Lynne Zucker, Michael Darby, and Marilynn B. Brewer, "Intellectual Human Capital and the Birth of U.S. Biotechnology Enterprises," *American Economic Review* 88 (1998): 290–306.

35. Robert H. Brockhaus, "The Psychology of the Entrepreneur," in *The Encyclopedia of Entrepreneurship*, eds.Calvin A. Kent, Donald L. Sexton, and Karl H. Vesper (Englewood Cliffs, NJ: Prentice Hall, 1982): 39–57.

36. Charles Handy, *Gods of Management: The Changing Work of Organizations* (New York: Random House, 1991).

37. Ibid.; Henry Mintzberg, Bruce Ahlstrand, and Joe Lampel, *Strategy Safari* (London: Prentice Hall, 1998).

38. Casson, *The Entrepreneur: An Economic Theory.*

Two

Entrepreneurs and Their World

In the previous chapter we said that an entrepreneur's primary resource is him/herself. We also defined entrepreneurship as "the process by which individuals, either on their own or inside organizations, pursue opportunities without regard to the resources they currently control." In this chapter we consider entrepreneurs and their world of resources, but not in the way that resources used to be considered in the economic and business literature; that is, as raw materials, capital, labor, and so on. Let us call it *human capital*, but not people as in labor but people as in *networks* and as *assets*. The central message of this chapter is that few entrepreneurs succeed working alone. Success is very much dependent on who the entrepreneur knows, what kind of relationships he or she has or are able to create, and why is it so important to maintain those relationships. Why is networking so crucial for the entrepreneur, when *self is the best serf*? It is critical to success. This chapter is about networks as much as it will be about building legitimacy and trust.

Drawing parallels to James Moore's work,[1] creating a new venture is like a new species entering an existing eco system or a new species creating a new eco system (which is often—but not always—the case in radical innovations and/or technology entrepreneurship). It can also be an existing species entering an existing eco system (replication). Most businesses belong to this latter category although they are not the ones that make media headlines. Surprisingly rare is an existing species slowly creating a new eco system, although it could be quite promising. A business eco system is a broader concept than the traditional industry as it can include a variety of interrelated industries. Conceptually, a business eco system incorporates the intense convergence of technologies and industries we have witnessed over the past two decades in both wireless and the Internet. Firms simultaneously cooperate and compete to develop innovative ideas, support new products, and satisfy customer needs en route to the next level of innovations. These often take place in various networks of activities at various levels—within firms, between firms, within regions, across regions, within nations, across nations, and so on. Business eco systems capture the boundary-crossing nature of today's dynamic business climate.

In the process of pursuing opportunities, one key task for the entrepreneur is to know how to draw on resources from the surrounding environment in order to purposefully coordinate resources thereby enabling purposeful action. In large organizations, there are routine mechanisms for scanning the environment and interacting with it, such as market intelligence, public relations, communications, sales, and so on. In a small firm, or when starting a small firm, there are no departments or routines for taking care of these matters. There is just the entrepreneur and, perhaps, a part-time office clerk (frequently a spouse). Yet this does not mean that these issues are not important or equally important to small firms as they are for large ones. They are probably even more important. However, there are not enough resources available.

Moreover, a small firm often lacks legitimacy and credibility in the eyes of most stakeholders, even potential employees. Beginning with getting a bank loan or credit from a supplier at reasonable terms is nearly impossible without credibility, legitimacy, and a *name*. It may be possible if the entrepreneur has a name from his or her previous worklife, for example, "He or she used to work in that organization," or "Oh, we know her, she is the very efficient secretary of the local tennis club." But what if you do not have a name and you have spotted a wonderful opportunity?

ENTREPRENEURIAL ENVIRONMENTS

Michael Porter of Harvard Business School showed that competition in an industry was determined by five forces: firm rivalry, bargaining power of suppliers, bargaining power of customers, new entrants, and possible substitute products or services. Competitive advantage was based on how well a firm excelled in managing its value chain and value system.[2] Along with rapid advances in technology (ICT and others) and globalization of business, these models of competitive advantage have increased in complexity. Our conceptualization of business environments is constantly evolving.

Firms are no longer national, but have transcended from international to transnational, multinational, and even global. In the United States, firms are increasingly facing competition from foreign firms at the same time as international markets are growing in importance even for small firms. In Europe, for example, the downfall of the Berlin Wall had widespread consequences for business. Also, as a consequence of the expansion of the European Union, many national and local firms realized that they faced competition from previously unknown actors. The rapid expansion of electronic commerce has further amplified globalization of business and the competitive eco system.

This expansion of markets presents the unprepared firm with real threats and others with massive business opportunities. Managing the business environment or external environment is as important for new small firms as it is for large established ones. Large organizations have dedicated departments or units to meet this challenge. Small and new firms have to solve this in a different way. First, entrepreneurs who are starting out must have an understanding of their business environment and the players in it. Then they have to learn to navigate in, and manage, that environment. The way to do this is through networking. But that is not a fast or a sufficient remedy. It takes time to create networks and it is an eternal chore for an entrepreneur.

Any firm, whether large or small, new or old, exists in a business environment (Figure 2.1), which has several layers and types of actors. The immediate environment includes customers, suppliers, and competitors providing substitute or complementary products or services. The immediate environment we still like to call the industry, although the boundaries of an industry have become increasingly blurred as previously separate industries converge as a result of technological convergence. But the firm and the industry exist in a larger environment, what we call here the business system. Figure 2.1 can also be seen as a representation of a firm's stakeholders. Stakeholders represent

FIGURE 2.1
The Business Environment, as Adapted from Moore

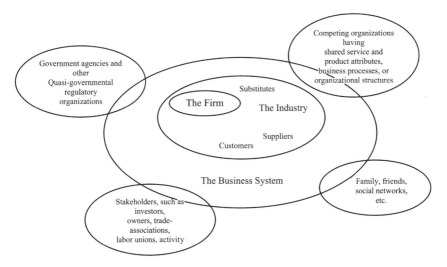

Source: James F. Moore, *The Death of Competition, Leadership Strategy in the Age of Business Ecosystems* (Hoboken, NJ: John Wiley & Sons, 1996).

FIGURE 2.2
Networked Sources of Information

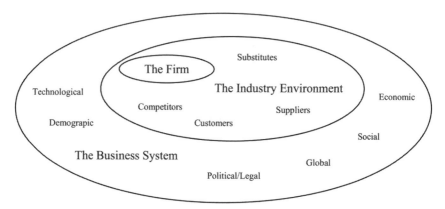

actors who form members of networks that an entrepreneur seeks to become part of or attempts to build. They represent sources of important information, or social capital, that a successful entrepreneur will need (Figure 2.2).

Some of this information can be acquired through purchasing commercial informational databases, but the content is often out of date. It may have the present date on the cover, but when analyzing the data one often finds that it is several years old (take census data, for example). Hence, a carefully crafted network can prove invaluable in providing fresh and relevant information or perspectives on existing information that provide insights into markets and opportunities. An entrepreneur needs to stay abreast with current information on the industry environment and that includes suppliers, customers, competitors, and others. However, an entrepreneur needs information from a wider perspective, at a macro level or business system perspective. Again, their network will serve as an important complement to newspapers, TV, and "googling" the Internet. It may seem trivial to mention this at all, but our experience is that many would-be entrepreneurs are poorly informed about vital issues in their business environment and fail to see the necessity for gathering information until it is too late. Therefore, we argue that information needs necessitates and justifies the importance for an entrepreneur to create and, above all, nurture a broad range of networks.

NETWORKS

The network is emerging as the signature form of organization in the Information Age, just as bureaucracy stamped the Industrial Age, hierarchy controlled the Agricultural Era, and the small group roamed in the Nomadic Era.[3]

With the emergence of the Internet and the World Wide Web, along with other sophisticated information and communications technology (ICT) solutions during the 1990s, the word *network* became a commodity in management parlance. The quote above is only one of them, but it does quite well capture the state of "flabbergastedness" many business people and researchers were caught in only some ten years ago. Technology was changing management if not revolutionizing it. Business was entering a new era, that of networks. Big businesses learned what small entrepreneurial firms were practicing daily. At that time networking became a management issue, an unprecedented managerial challenge. Many consultants saw their businesses flourishing.

The above quote also nicely presents us with a model for the different stages entrepreneurial firms may pass through in their development, or, as will be explained here, the many forms in which they will exist simultaneously. A small firm may seem like a small group roaming the wilderness, but at the same time it is building the necessary networks while trying to avoid creating a bureaucracy or a hierarchy.

Regardless of whether the firm is small or large, new or old, there are certain minimum requirements for a network to be a business network of any use. Networks are not self-perpetuating, they need to be created and nurtured. Any amount of ICT, no matter how sophisticated, will not alone make a network successful. A Web site does not make a network, nor is it made out of luck. As a bare necessity, networks require purpose, members, and links.[4] Members and links are physical, purpose and relationships are intangible or imaginary (Figure 2.3).

FIGURE 2.3
A Network Anatomy

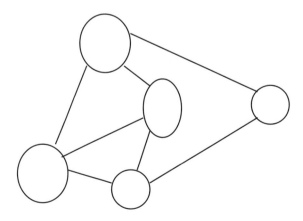

- Purpose is an expressed unifying aim and a set of values shared by the members.
- Members are those individuals and groups (can be firms) that contribute specific capabilities to achieve a shared purpose.
- Links connect members through relationships, repetitive interaction, and physical ties.

ENTREPRENEURIAL NETWORKS

While much of the knowledge of the entrepreneur can be classified as "know-how," perhaps the most important part, and the hardest to quantify, is "know-who." The major factors distinguishing a successful entrepreneur from an unsuccessful one are the *quality* and *vitality* of their personal networks. The fact that an entrepreneur is a member of a network is not key, but the quality and vitality of the network are. It should be added that successful entrepreneurs most likely belong to many networks that have been purposefully chosen, based on the purpose.

To be blunt, entrepreneurs are best when they have a few good friends and a lot of acquaintances. We are not suggesting that entrepreneurs are gregarious, but if meeting with other often unknown people, talking about oneself, and telling other people why they should believe in you are perceived as problematic, it will be necessary to get over them. One entrepreneur who became very successful described how he overcame his shyness: "But, this was really hard for me—I had never been good with telling how good I was, so I had cold sweat on my forehead every time. I really overcame a tremendous personal psychological barrier here. I still feel like 'whoa' when I think about it. But, boy was it hard."

Networking, the ability to build networks or developing value-adding contacts is a learned behavior. Some of us may possess personal qualities from birth, but in principle, shyness and any disposition with public appearances can be "trained away." For example, language skills are critical in networking, and that is all about learning.

Unlike successful professionals in most careers where a strong mentoring relationship is critical, we have learned that the strength of the entrepreneur lies in the diversity and reach of their networks. Networks are literally the keys to entrepreneurial success. We are here referring to personal, trust-building relationships. This is a lot more than going to local entrepreneurs' meetings and engaging in small talk over cocktails, or even the act of "exchanging business card." Cocktails and business cards are artifacts, where the latter contains goods that have information. In the process of building real value-adding networks, it is extremely important to understand that this will take place only if the other member perceives you as a potential or actual value-adding member to his or her network.

We know that networks are complex and loosely connected. We also know that entrepreneurs build highly diverse networks that are more stable than their firms and that networks are built over time. It is also important to note that networks are personal, not institutional, and will outlast any specific venture. This is one reason that, for example, succession in family business can be a very tricky thing or a change of a CEO in a small firm may be equally tricky. It is especially hard to transfer networks.

This simply means that one does not acquire a network by going to a certain school or joining an organization, but one does sow the seeds of potentially very strong and meaningful networks. We tell our students on a daily basis that they are in fact cultivating future networks while studying at universities or going to association meetings.

When building networks it is necessary to actively work at getting to know people and their needs, wants, and fears. It is also known that the real strength of an entrepreneur's network is what is called the "strength of weak ties."[5] That is, it is not who you know that counts, but who your network knows that you do not (Figure 2.4). Entrepreneurs build networks and relationships in a conscious and proactive process. We know that entrepreneurs may spend half of their time developing new contacts and managing old ones. That is, networking is a time-consuming activity, and in a situation with scarce resources there is a real risk of loosing it all. For a start-up entrepreneur it can be quite overwhelming. This is what we call the risk of overdeterminism. When networking, one is in fact doing multiple tasks associated with the venture, such as marketing and fund raising. Otherwise, there will not be enough hours in the

FIGURE 2.4
The Strength of the Weak Ties

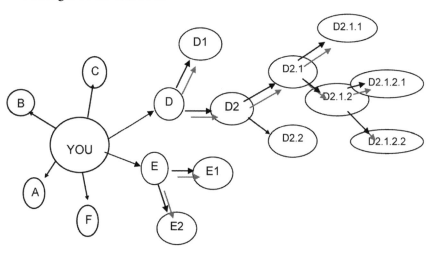

day to be effective. Hence networking is as much about organizing the venture and the activities as building relationships. This is why the members one seeks into the network or the membership of a network one seeks to join have to share the purpose or contribute to reaching the goals with the venture.

For any entrepreneur, whether start-up or already established, there are a few obvious sources for engaging a network. Below are examples of these sources. (The structure of entrepreneurial networks is shown in Figure 2.5.)

- Formal and informal liaisons with suppliers and wholesalers
- Contracts or informal relationships with subcontractors
- Existing contracts with potential customers or clients
- Potential clients through networks established in prior employment
- Attorneys
- Certified public accountants
- Consulting organizations
- Research scientists or engineers
- Import/export brokers
- Family
- Realtors

It is often said, by would-be entrepreneurs and others, that the only really critical resource needed is money. But it is known that networks are often the

FIGURE 2.5
Entrepreneurial Networks

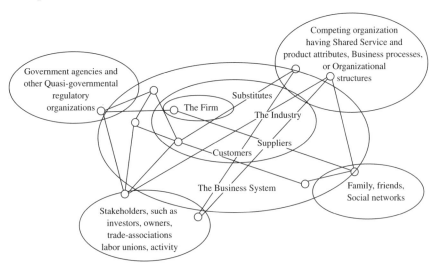

source of funding. While money is often needed, most companies start out with hardly any assets whatsoever. In Finland the minimum amount of money needed to start a limited company is €8,000, and in the United States a majority of firms have started with less than US$5,000.[6] Larger amounts of start-up capital are needed for firms with intentions to grow and hire employees.[7]

What most people forget is that financial resources are certainly one of those instances where networks play an important role in acquiring funding. In fact networks may be the difference between acquiring funds or not. People invest in people as much as they do in good ideas or business concepts. One should never forget that funds are invested not just because the concept of the venture is worth it but also because they believe that the people running the firm can execute the plan. Building relationships early, before they are needed, with bankers, security analysts, savings and loan managers, investment fund managers, insurance companies, venture capitalists, and certainly private (angel) investors is critical. Even noninvestors can be gatekeepers to the people with funds. Moreover, financial resources can come from any number of "nonfinancial" members of the network. People invest in either the entrepreneur or the idea. This is the power of the strength of weak ties. Does the entrepreneur belong to any professional association? These are important networking resources within the industry.

What many individuals do not recognize as important sources of relationships (until too late) are various types of organizational relationships, such as with previous employers and universities that may be valuable to the venture. Other types of organizational relationships are formal ties with corporations through new venture units, ties to government agencies (for SBIR grants in the United States or TEKES in Finland), state agencies, and local political organizations. Most entrepreneurs we know have relationships with both the parties in power and those in opposition. One needs to be always in a position to both know what is going on and influence decisions. A highly successful female entrepreneur in India who supported the Congress Party once commented on a possible regime shift: "[W]hat makes you think we don't keep good friends in the BJP?"

Most individuals also consider social relationships equally important, such as those from memberships in local, state, or national service associations like Rotary, their local church, synagogue or mosque, or business organizations like the Chamber of Commerce. We meet people while attending trade and professional conferences, or even on the plane traveling to those events. Important relationships can be established through local or regional social clubs, community organizations, athletic clubs, and social events. Relationships can begin because of newspaper article about the entrepreneur that brings those interested into contact with that person. It is obvious that building the network is a life-long process and one cannot build a good network overnight. It is important to remember that building networks is a means to an end.

Finally, we have often been struck by how entrepreneurs vary in the use of an obvious source of network resources: family and friendship networks through family ties. We have seen those who exploit this source vigorously while others avoid it like the plague. Certainly, there is a price to pay when using family relationships (as we know family guilt is the gift that keeps on giving). But to ignore this as an avenue to needed resources is as foolish as it is to ignore ethnic, cultural, and religious affiliations or fraternal organizations.

NETWORK IN CONTEXT

Earlier in this chapter we stated that networks were propelled into the wider business consciousness during the 1990s. One of the key technological contributors to this development was the Internet, the Web, and, obviously, significant advances in ICT. But networks have been around as long as there have been tribes, clans, social clubs, and business groups like Chambers of Commerce. However, something else was taking place in recent times. Society and economies were transcending into knowledge-based economies.[8] Staying abreast with advances in knowledge became a key to business and personal success. On a business level, the increased dependency on advances in knowledge was perhaps most visible in research and development. Previously, firms had performed their R&D activities in-house, and R&D had been regarded as proprietary knowledge unique and rare enough to be kept in-house. With intensified advances in knowledge creation this fully integrated R&D model began to crumble. It was economically impossible to create new knowledge at sustainable speed in-house. Sourcing R&D in specialized R&D networks became the new way to operate. In fact, this development started before the Internet, and it is fair to say that both, when their paths crossed in the early 1990s, had stunning consequences for the networked economy.

While this has happened in a number of industrial sectors, we are specifically referring to advances in biotechnology, which changed the way several industries operate, perhaps most profoundly the pharmaceutical industry. It changed the norm of fully integrated R&D—but incrementally—into network-based R&D, where some is performed within universities, some within small biotechnology firms, and some in contract research organizations. Even venture capitalists and ICT companies are involved in the biotechnology R&D process and ultimately a traditional big pharma (Figure 2.6). This model is seen as today's norm. Yet, involving so many parties may save some resources but expand the need for others. One chief R&D officer complained

FIGURE 2.6
Network-based R&D in Biotechnology

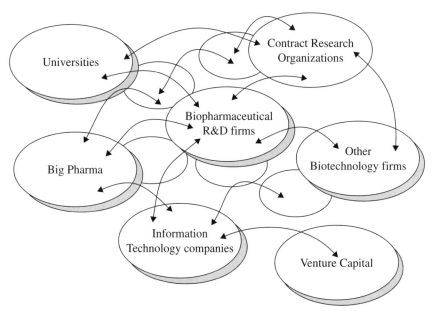

that they had to hire nine persons into quality control to ensure that every subcontractor met quality requirements.

It all started in November 1973 when an article by Stanley Cohen and Herbert Boyen was published. The article reported on the scientific break-through of recombinant DNA and is commonly regarded as the genesis of modern biotechnology. The commercial break-through took place on October 14, 1980 when Genentech went public and listed their stock on the US stock exchange. The firm, which had been founded a few years earlier and employed some 20 persons, had gone from small-scale protein production for R&D purpose to large-scale production for commercial purposes. What happened that day, in October nobody had been able to anticipate. Genentech was going to sell one million shares for $35 a piece. An outrageous idea in itself since the company did not have product even near the horizon before 1984. That is, they were selling hope. And, boy did HOPE sell. Within 20 minutes the stock price sold at $89 a piece and ended at $70. In 24 hours the market capitalization of the firm had doubled. Not only was the market behaviour stunning, but also the firms and their operations: no products and managed by researchers out of the university labs, with no previous business management experience.[9]

Genentech opened up the industry for the knowledge-based and network-based economy, and others followed suit. The network-based business model is not exactly proven as of yet as there are less than 100 profitable biotech companies worldwide to date, although there are more than 5,000 biotechnology firms in the United States and Europe pursuing success. But we believe there is no return to the fully integrated R&D model either. Networks have clearly impacted new firms in a new industry.

Today, networks are critical in technology- and science-based entrepreneurship. Networks are closely connected to knowledge management, organizational learning, and both the formal and informal networks associated with R&D. In a wider perspective, on a macro level networks are connected to technology incubators, industrial clusters, and science parks. Innovative activities seen as complex research are as much based on existing knowledge as on creating new. This suggests that for an entrepreneur, innovations management is an interfirm as much as an intrafirm activity. Networks are therefore critical to the technology entrepreneur. They are also critical to the nontechnology entrepreneur. A restaurant concept needs innovation, technology, and networks to succeed as well.

In the rapidly changing business environments, factors such as technological and regulatory uncertainties, ambiguous markets, high development costs, and unbalanced competitive structures are challenges that must be addressed. Uncertainty pervades in any new venture, technology-based ones in particular. At the outset of a project, assessments of costs, duration, and outcomes are virtually impossible and uncertainties of research can only be resolved as the project progresses. However, the same might well be said for most start-ups, even a restaurant. Since it is almost impossible to forecast which technologies and products will make their way through the markets and become success stories, it is necessary to combat this uncertainty. Many entrepreneurs establish multiple interorganizational linkages, or networks, in early phases. Restaurants do not necessarily create new technologies, but they are constantly on the look out for better ways to control costs and improve efficiencies. Just look at the use of technology in any national brand fast-food establishment.

Thus, the locus of innovation is in networks of entrepreneurs and their firms as a group, rather than individual firms. An entrepreneur's collaborations are both a resource and a signal to markets and stakeholders of the quality of their firm's activities. A new venture's set of alliances influences its innovative capabilities as well as others' perceptions of its capabilities. Networks provide resource sharing, allowing firms to combine knowledge, skills, and assets. Collaborative linkages provide access to knowledge spillovers, serving as information conduits through which new insights to problems travel from one firm to another. The number of direct ties to external collaborators positively affects a firm's innovative output by providing knowledge sharing, complementary skills, and scale.

REGIONAL AND NATIONAL ENVIRONMENTS
SUPPORTING ENTREPRENEURSHIP

The networks in which entrepreneurs exist are boundary crossing; they cross not only organizational boundaries but also industrial, regional, and national boundaries. This means that most organizations, whether large or small, operate in multiple environments simultaneously. The disciplines of economic geography and marketing are the ones in which location problems are studied in depth. From the perspective of entrepreneurship, the issue of location and its contribution to business success sprung into a wider consciousness with the initial success of Silicon Valley and Route 128 in the mid-1970s.[10] Although both areas experienced a slow down, from which Route 128 did not manage to recuperate until much later, these two areas became role models for similar type of technology-based agglomerations worldwide.

In many countries, programs to create similar regional agglomerations were initiated. It was argued that entrepreneurship and regions of entrepreneurial and innovative vitality would significantly contribute to economic wealth creation (with specific reference to Silicon Valley). There is a massive body of research on entrepreneurship, innovation, national and regional innovation systems, "science parks," "research parks," "technology centers," "innovation centers," "incubator centers," "start-up initiatives," and "business parks." Between 1987 and 2002 over 200 articles have been published, and there is no decline in the level of interest toward the issue in sight.[11] Literature shows the usefulness of national innovation systems (NIS) for institutions devoted to innovation.[12] What is important to realize here is that the core of NIS is interrelated institutions, or networked institutions, that is, those members that produce, diffuse, and adapt new technological knowledge, such as industrial firms, universities, or government agencies. Typically, governmental agencies, the city itself and the surrounding municipalities as well as the universities are strong actors in setting up these institutions.[13] National and regional innovation systems are seen as networked learning systems of national economies. Often used key words are innovation networks, infrastructure, globalization, asymmetric knowledge, dynamics capability, knowledge spillovers, technology transfer, region, sector, national innovation policy, and so on.

Research has also shown that proximity-based networks of R&D institutions showed that small firms emerging in close proximity to world-class science institutions are more successful.[14] Interestingly, research also shows that top scientists working in close proximity to start-up technology firms become better scientists because they ask better questions early in their careers and become highly cited ones.

One model of regional and national innovation systems that has gained increasing adherents is the Triple Helix perspective,[15] which seeks a way for government, universities, and industry to interact in an effective network. Although criticized by Cooke as being on an extremely high level of abstraction,[16] it is a model that many NIS of today appear to be based on. For example, the Swedish national body for promoting innovation and technology, VINNOVA, openly declares that their system is based on Triple Helix. In Finland regional centers of excellence (there are twenty-two such centers) are said to be based on Triple Helix.

While considerable efforts have been made, results in terms of increased entrepreneurship have not been the outcome of these network-based structures. In fact several studies show that government intervention may become counterproductive; that is, they reduce value rather than adding value for the individual firm. It appears that regions and nations indeed can support entrepreneurship, but what the real effects of government intervention are is far from clear. We still lack adequate responses to questions like these: What kinds of incentives can governments create for regions to encourage entrepreneurship? What kind of incentives would cause entrepreneurs to relocate their business?

Nevertheless, these incentive and support programs exist and we leave it to the individual entrepreneurs to decide for themselves which one to use or to keep from using. In the United States there are both federal and state programs and their equivalents exist in Europe as well. While there are multiple types of incentives available, they fundamentally fall into the following categories:

- Regional development grants
- Incubator programs
- Employee training programs
- Selective financial assistance
- Rent or rate subsidy
- Subsidized loans
- Venture capital investment
- Income tax reduction
- Property tax reduction
- Fixed asset tax reduction

Different incentive packages may be beneficial at different stages of the firm's life cycle. It is advisable to anticipate at what point the firm will be independent of these incentives. Any decision about incentives should also be tempered with the simple fact, is this where the entrepreneur wants to live and locate his or her business regardless of the value of these incentives? To be blunt, can the entrepreneur build the kinds of networks in a specific location that will support his or her firm once the firm is no longer eligible to receive governmental support? Finally, it may be worth considering what impact incentives can have on the image of an entrepreneurial firm, or, for example, a new not-for-profit venture. The entrepreneur has also to consider how complicated the incentive process will be in terms of application as well as reporting. Are the benefits real or is it much ado about nothing?

Given below are some practical advice on how to build networks for supporting a venture in the making:

- Realize that this is going to take time and energy as well as money.
- Be proactive and willing to meet people. It also means that the entrepreneur will have to be a bit Machiavellian while building the networks.
- It is fine to use people and manipulate them if one remembers to give them what they want as well. That way they will be around to be used again. If one is selfish, the network will most likely not be effective.
- Start reading regularly a local newspaper (including electronic news) and keep up with the national and international arenas.

Staying informed is a cheap insurance against changes in the environment. The strength of weak signals is as important as the strength of weak ties as told by a major entrepreneur in construction management:

Ten years ago I began to prepare for what is increasingly becoming a shortage of cement and construction steel: It was based on my assessment of the rapid growth of Chinese cities as reported in the news and by my friends abroad. I knew that would have an impact on building in south Florida just as much as the hurricanes do.

ELEVEN COMMANDMENTS FOR ENTREPRENEURIAL VALUE-ADDED CONTACTS

A number of years ago Dr. Rein Peterson, one of the "grand old men" of academic entrepreneurship in Canada, and Dr. Robert Ronstadt, his colleague in the United States, shared with one of the authors their secrets for understanding the network phenomena in entrepreneurs. To these a grandfather's wisdom has been added. We call them the eleven commandments of networking (Moses was given Ten Commandments, entrepreneurs get eleven).

- Commandment 1: Know-who is as important as entrepreneurial know-how. Be diplomatic, do not let development of contacts that will assist you in starting your new venture constrain you.

- Commandment 2: Be systematic, explicit, and proactive in creating and managing your network. It is important to remember that value-added contacts are often invisible. Remember the strength of weak ties as discussed above.

- Commandment 3: Always assess your contacts in terms of the specific type of venture you are starting. Use your judgment and stay focused. It is important to remember that high growth ventures require high growth networks.

- Commandment 4: Locate your business venture geographically to take optimum advantage of your contacts and to maximize the growth of your contacts as it relates to your venture.

- Commandment 5: The strengths and weaknesses of your personal contacts become apparent only when they are used. Once again, remember the concept of the "strength of weak ties."

- Commandment 6: Identify and communicate continuously with the gatekeepers in your network. Remember, if you do not use it, you will lose it. Who are the gatekeepers in your network?

- Commandment 7: Always assess your entrepreneurial contacts not just in terms of traditional business or industry attributes, but also in terms of entrepreneurial functions and needs.

- Commandment 8: Contribute your own value-added contacts. Share, and it will be returned.

- Commandment 9: If possible, use some kind of device to keep, track, sort, and classify the relationship you have as value-added contacts. Trying to please everybody is a recipe for failure.

- Commandment 10: Do not become a slave to developing your value-added contacts. Show passion, not obsession.

- Granddad Jones' 11th Commandment: It is not *what* you know that counts, but *who* you know. But if you do not know the what, the who will not talk to you.

NOTES

    1. James F. Moore, *The Death of Competition, Leadership Strategy in the Age of Business Ecosystems* (Hoboken, NJ: John Wiley & Sons, 1996).

    2. Michael E. Porter, *Competitive Advantage* (New York: The Free Press, 1985); Porter, *Competitive Strategy* (New York: The Free Press, 1980).

    3. Jessica Lipnack and Jeffrey Stamps, *The Age of the Network: Organizing Principles for the 21st Century* (Essex Junction, VT: Omneo, 1994).

    4. Ibid.; Lipnack and Stamps, *The TeamNet Factor: Bringing the Power of Boundary Crossing into the Heart of Your Business* (Essex Junction, VT: Oliver Wight Publications, 1993); Lipnack and Stamps, *Virtual Teams: Reaching across Space, Time, and Organizations with Technology* (Hoboken, NJ: John Wiley & Sons, 1997).

    5. Mark S. Granovetter, "Economic Action and Social Structure: The Problem of Embeddedness," *The American Sociological Review* 91 (1985): 481–510; Granovetter, "The Strength of Weak Ties," *The American Journal of Sociology* 78 (1973): 1362–1380.

6. Howard E. Aldrich and Martha A. Martinez, "Many Are Called, but Few Are Chosen: An Evolutionary Perspective for the Study of Entrepreneurship," *Entrepreneurship Theory & Practice* 24 (2001): 41–56.

7. William Bygrave and William Hunt, GEM 2004 Financing Report, 2005. www.gem-consortium.org.

8. Peter F. Drucker, "The New Society of Organizations," *Harvard Business Review* 70 (1992): 95–105.

9. Cynthia Robbins-Roth, *From Alchemy to IPO* (Cambridge, MA: Perseus Publishing, 2000); Richard W. Oliver, *The Coming of the Biotech Age* (New York: McGraw Hill, 2000).

10. Annalee Saxenian, *Regional Advantage: Culture and Competition in Silicon Valley and Route 128* (Cambridge: Harvard University Press, 1994).

11. Harald Bathelt, "Regional Competence and Economic Recovery: Divergent Growth Paths in Boston's High Technology Economy," *Entrepreneurship & Regional Development* 13 (2001): 287–314; Phil Cooke, "Regional Assymetric Knowledge Capabilities and Open Innovation. Exploring 'Globalisation 2'—A New Model of Industry Organisation," *Research Policy* 34 (2005): 1128–1149; Alain Thierstein and Beate Wilhelm, "Incubator, Technology, and Innovations Centres in Switzerland: Features and Policy Implications," *Entrepreneurship & Regional Development* 13 (2001): 315–331.

12. Chris Freeman, "Continental, National and Sub-national Innovation Systems—Complementarity and Economic Growth," *Research Policy* 31 (2002): 191–211; Richard R. Nelson, "National Innovation Systems: A Retrospective on a Study," *Industrial and Corporate Change* 1 (1992): 347–374; Jorge Niosi, "National Systems of Innovation Are 'X-efficient' (and X-effective). Why Some Are Slow Learners," *Research Policy* 31 (2002): 291–302.

13. Alan L. Carsrud and Bradley B. Ellison, "Turning Academic Research into Enterprise: An Exploratory Study of the United Kingdom," in *Managing Organizational Transitions in a Global Economy*, ed. Richard M. Schwartz (Los Angeles: Institute of Industrial Relations/UCLA Press, 1992), 119–148.

14. Lynne G. Zucker, Michael R. Darby, and Jeff S. Armstrong, "Commercializing Knowledge: University Science, Knowledge Capture, and Firm Performance in Biotechnology," *Management Science* 48 (2002): 138–153; Lynne G. Zucker, Michael R. Darby, and Marilynn B. Brewer, "Intellectual Human Capital and the Birth of U.S. Biotechnology Enterprises," *American Economic Review* 88 (1998): 290–306.

15. Henry Etzkowitz and Loet Leydesdorff, "The Dynamics of Innovation: From National Systems and 'Mode 2' to a Triple Helix of University-Industry-Government Relations," *Research Policy* 29 (2000): 109–123.

16. Cooke, "Regional Assymetric Knowledge. Exploring 'Globalisation 2.'"

PART II

BUILDING THE BUSINESS

Three

Idea Generation and Creating the Concept Statement

This chapter deals with what we consider the very core of entrepreneurship: How do some discover opportunities and others do not? How are the opportunities evaluated, and how are concepts developed for exploiting those opportunities? This chapter provides some idea-generation exercises and methods for rapid screening of opportunities for potential new ventures. The key is to exploit the best opportunities that fit your specific goals, desires, and passions. It is also necessary to conduct both a conceptual and a technical feasibility analysis.[1]

This chapter reviews how to describe a business idea and how to develop appropriate business strategies and revenue models for a business concept. Critical to this process is to begin to write down the business concept and start on an executive summary for a business plan to execute that concept. Real examples of business concept statements and of executive summaries of a business plan are provided. As a final exercise the reader is asked to do a five-minute "elevator pitch" that will answer "What are you doing and why would anybody give you money for it?"

One way of approaching the issue of idea generation is to consider what motivates people. Put simply, there are three things that motivate people's actions and, interestingly, these can also be seen as sources of opportunities for an entrepreneur. People have needs, wants, and fears. In marketing, students are taught to focus on customer needs and wishes, and anyone capable of providing something that will match customers' needs and wants will be successful. However, we think it is also important to look at the other side of the coin, that is, *fear*, as alleviating fear offers a whole range of business opportunities. Just look at the entire insurance industry. Stated differently, people *need* transportation, they *want* a Bentley, and they *fear* getting stuck in public transportation in most American cities. The *need* will state the benefit sought for and the *want* will state the desired core product or service. In another city somewhere else in the world, the answers might be entirely different. For example, there is a need for transportation—to meet for lunch—in Stockholm. To get quickly from one place to another, say, from the Royal Institute of Technology to the indoor marketplace in Östermalm, the famous Östermalmshallarna, one way would be to take a car or take public transportation, that is, the underground. But that would not be fast transportation at all. The solution here would be to take a bike and pray for no rain! Needs, wants, and fears are clearly situational as well as individual.

Hence entrepreneurs should be able to express the business idea by quickly stating what needs they are addressing, what wants they are fulfilling, or what fears they are relieving. This is also the rationale or the recipe for creating an "elevator pitch" or three-minute presentation of the business concept. It should be possible to tie it to addressing a need, want, or fear.

IDEA GENERATION AS PROBLEM SOLVING AND FOCUS

When discussing means of discovering opportunities or finding a viable business idea, it is necessary to remember that what is perceived as an opportunity or a good idea by one person may not be perceived so by another. That is, opportunities are in the eyes of the beholder. Therefore, we offer here a number of guiding questions for anyone to ask himself or herself when "thinking that he or she may have recognized an opportunity." This will help anyone interested in developing a viable business concept. Opportunity recognition, as we see it, is essentially a process involving several steps.

Opportunity recognition is the process of applying a number of problem-solving techniques. This means that asking the right question is much more important than finding the right answer very fast. A good way to start is to ask "What would my customers want if they knew they could get it?" Or, many can surely think of situations where one has thought "that service should be significantly improved." Thinking of ways to improve a service or a product can be a perfect business idea. This search process is sometimes referred to as thinking "out of the box," that is, to question the normal way of doing something. It requires that regular assumptions about ordinary procedures are unbundled. And this is important, especially since what is seen as the *normal* way to do something may not be the *best* way, given changes in customers or technology.

For example, Sam Walton realized that it was not necessary to have distributors who only added to the costs of goods. Additionally, most retailers at that time also ignored rural areas because they were perceived less profitable.

Wal-Mart was the result of Sam Walton thinking out of the box or his discovering problems for which he had very good solutions.

The success of Southwest Airlines was not that it flew a unique aircraft, but how it organized itself to capture the market by providing services people wanted and could afford, through point-to-point service with one type of aircraft. Equally good examples are Starbucks Coffee and McDonalds.

Quite often, divergent or imaginative thinkers tend to notice opportunities or problems. One of the keys to developing divergent thinking is not to constrain yourself with predefined solutions to the problems you see. That is, when you have a "hammer, everything is perceived as a nail." While curiosity and attention are certainly essential for noticing what is wrong and what could be an opportunity, the key to any entrepreneurial venture is *focus, focus, and focus.* Thinking differently about reality can be seen as much a process of focusing as a process of unraveling the iceberg:

- Learn to define the issue as more than is immediately visible.
- Go beyond the symptoms to the core issue.
- Isolate what you are looking for and focus on what is the underlying issue or problem.
- Engage the problem and search for information. Good entrepreneurs create an expertise in data gathering.
- Find pertinent facts and do not ignore the information that is contradictory to expectations.
- Analyze data and use well-established logical models, but remember that comprehension means knowing something is right before it can be consciously explained. Therefore, blend facts with your own intuition. While it is important to make use of prior training and education, it is equally important not to be constrained by it.
- Accept that this process is not going to be easy.
- Engage yourself with the problem and feel passionate about solving it.
- Expect uncertainty.

One often-used idea-generating method is brainstorming. Through brainstorming it is possible to generate a large quantity of possible solutions to problems. But this may also create the uncertainty of choice; that is, which alternative to choose. At this point it is perfectly appropriate to let ideas incubate, to allow time for the ideas to hatch or ferment. The difficulty here is to hurry slowly; that is, one should not wait too long, either. While timing is always critical it is a fact that even entrepreneurs need time to think. However, that time is rarely given; it has to be taken.

Many marketing and strategy textbooks have for years claimed that first to market is the key to success. But, it is *first to market acceptance* that is critical. Osborne was the first to develop the personal computer, but how many remember ever hearing that? IBM was the first to market acceptance, and the rest is one big success story now dominated by Michael Dell's firm.

DEVELOPING THE CONCEPT

When developing a concept it is necessary to first clarify what the business is, that is, what the purpose is. According to one of the most influential thinkers in management, Peter Drucker, the *purpose of a business is to create a customer*. Drucker claimed this in 1954, half a century ago! Yet, this seems to be one of the hardest truths in business to get across. In other words, it is not profit, innovation, or total quality management. It is *to create a customer*. Profitability is a necessary requirement, but not the purpose. With no customers, there will be no need to produce products, so no profit and no problems with creating shareholder value because there is NOTHING.

So how does the firm create a customer? Drucker answers, "through marketing and innovation."[2] When writing a business plan, what really takes place is a formalization process of the business concept of how to create a customer. The business concept is the business model that proves it is possible to create a market with effective demand, that there are customers willing to pay. A viable business model requires a sound revenue model, with one objective—to be profitable. Again, according to Drucker, profit is the test of the validity of the business model or the concept. More importantly, profit is a condition of survival, the cost of the future, the cost of staying in business.

Business plans are not only written for funders and venture capitalists. Actually, we think it is first and foremost a tool for the entrepreneur as a means to clarify to himself or herself what the business is, should be, and will be. It is an analysis, organizing, and communication tool. Writing a business plan is a process that justifies the venture; it is a feasibility study and a blue print. The business plan and the process of developing the business concept should provide answers to the following questions:

- What is the business of your firm?
- What is your business really?
- What will your business become?
- What is your firm trying to accomplish?
- What do your customers think your firm is trying to accomplish?
- Do you know how you are doing and where you are going?

Developing a concept and ultimately a business plan for activating the concept is like imagining the venture five years ahead into the future. But it is an imagination process that is based on facts rather than pink dreams. While the concept statement, which is short and concise, is the key part in a business plan it is also the key for the entire venture. If the concept statement is blurry it is highly likely that the entire idea is equally fuzzy. The plan is a formalization of your imagination exercise—the five-year future vision. What is it? What should it be? How will you get there? Good questions to ask are

- What customer needs, wants, and fears are presently going unaddressed?
- Will requirements of present customers change?
- What new end-user applications are likely to emerge?
- What new technologies will be used to meet unmet needs of customer groups?
- What will competitors do and what difference will that make?
- What customer needs and customer groups should the organization be getting in position to serve?

But there are more questions to be asked in the process of concept development. What should be created? What could be created by this firm? Is this firm capable of implementing that creation? Is it possible to envision the concept and the firm in this development process one year, three years, and five years ahead? While this is not the concept statement, it is an image of the mental activities involved in the process of developing the concept statement. The result should be a concept expressed in no more than four sentences in nontechnical language. That is, *Tell me what it is you are trying to do and why would anyone give you money for it.*

The difference between a concept statement and a mission statement is very small. The significant difference is perhaps that a concept statement tells people what a venture is like before it exists.

For the benefit of the reader we have created a question checklist. Our experience from teaching entrepreneurship and helping to write business plans have taught us that writing a business plan is as much a scientific process as it is an artistic one. We claim that there is no single way to write a plan but there are a lot of ways to do it wrong. Therefore, these questions are beneficial. They will help the entrepreneur and the management team create a common understanding of what should be done and what they want to do.

The checklist of questions is for each section of the plan. It is not a fill-in-the-blanks exercise. Some questions may be relevant for the venture and some may not be. It is for the entrepreneur to determine which they are. Since it is important that the business plan is written by the entrepreneur and not a consultant or somebody else, these questions are here to help in that process. Think of the answers to the questions as a set of statements.

The Concept Checklist or the Elevator Pitch

1. Define the important and distinct functions of the product/service.
   Domino's distinct feature was its delivery, not its pizza.
2. What are the unique or proprietary aspects of the product/service?
   Are there patents, formula, brand name, copyright, trademark, and the like?
3. Describe any innovative technology involved with the product/service.
   What is new or different (e.g., electric toothbrush, unique organizational structure, new production techniques).
4. Describe the position the concept plays in the industry.
   Manufacturing, distributor/wholesaler, retailer, and so on.
5. Who is the intended customer or customer group?
   Who will pay for the products or services?
   Who makes the decision?
   Who will use the products or services?
6. What benefits will be delivered to the customer?
   What problems are you solving for your customer? (e.g., people buy 1/4" holes, not 1/4" drill bits).
7. How will the product/service be sold to the customer?
   Retail stores, direct sales, manufacturers representatives, telemarketing, distributors, franchising, Internet, strategic alliance.
8. Who will make the product or design the service?
   Subcontractor; in-house, home-base contractors; outsourced; and others.
9. How will the customer know you exist?
   How will they become aware of you?

All this may sound very easy, but it is not. The trick is doing it in one paragraph containing no more than four sentences. Get some paper and try to do this for the business! From years of work and research we have found it will take approximately thirty versions to get it down to something that is easily understood by others. The value of this exercise is that once it has been done it is easy to respond to someone in, for example, an elevator when they ask what your business is about or what you do—*the elevator pitch.*

CONCEPT STATEMENT EXERCISE

Consider this somewhat lengthy concept statement:
La Mexican Topical Café is interested in developing land on Sapphire Drive in Weston, Florida. Our business concept is a High End Mexican Restaurant. The design will create a dining experience that can be reproduced

in a franchise format. Familiar Mexican fare will be presented in a gourmet adaptation. We will bring an elegant overtone to the party atmosphere generally associated with a Mexican Restaurant. Beyond the gourmet appeal, another significant menu component will be meals tailored to fit current trends in dieting (Atkins, South Beach). This is to serve the dieter who wants to eat out in an excellent venue without destroying their dietary goals. In order to tap the market of folks who would like to drink but are constrained by a diet, this "on a diet" menu will include "low- to no-carb" alcoholic beverages like "Bacardi and no-carb Coke" or drinks made with Splenda instead of sugar.

Rewrite this concept and shorten it so that it is more exciting or appealing to readers. Are all details in here necessary?

THE EXECUTIVE SUMMARY

While the entire business plan is a more detailed version of the business concept, the Executive Summary is the concise version of the same. It is vital that the Executive Summary is well written, as in many cases this is the only part that is read by outsiders, such as funders. The Executive Summary is a "Readers' Digest" of your business plan and what your business concept is. As this section in most cases is the only one that gets read it is usually the part that gets the least amount of attention. That is, it is written last and in great haste. We firmly recommend the following procedure:

Write it first and continuously; that is, start with it, but for each section, like marketing and competition, that is subsequently developed in the full business plan, the revise the Executive Summary. Each time the Executive Summary will be improved, and this is to our minds the best kind of a guarantee that there will not be any discrepancies between the Executive Summary and the business plan.

Under no circumstances should you write it last as a cut-and-paste version of the plan.

The Executive Summary can be seen as an outline of the entrepreneur's strategic thinking. This is the part of the documented business concept that needs to stand on its own. The concept statement is one paragraph of the Executive Summary and if presented as a PowerPoint slide presentation, it is one early slide. For your benefit we offer you once again a checklist—this time for the Executive Summary.

Executive Summary Checklist

1. State the purpose of the business: retail, manufacturing, distributor, service, or others.

2. Describe the current stage of development for the venture: start-up, initial operations, expansion, rapid growth, stable operations, acquisition, turnaround, or new product.

3. Describe what is unique about the product/service. List any proprietary rights the business has (patents, licenses, royalties, distribution rights, franchise agreements, and others).

4. What form of organization will the business operate under: proprietorship, partnership, LLC, limited partnership, S-corporation, or corporation.

5. Define and highlight key management personnel. What are their skills that will help the new venture. List existing and potential management team members. Complete resumes of existing management team members should be placed in the appendix.

6. Describe and highlight the key support groups for your management team: accountants, attorneys, consultants, Board of Directors, Advisory Council.

7. Describe briefly the following: industry, customer, customer needs, product benefits, target markets, market penetration plan. In other words, give the reader an overview of the marketing plan.

8. Describe your major competitors: who is your direct competition, who is your indirect competition, what are their strengths and weaknesses.

9. How much money does the venture need: for product development, marketing, and operations. Highlight how much money is needed to get started and how it will be spent.

10. How long will it take for the business to break-even: explain how long will it take this venture to turn a profit. Break-even is the level of sales at which total revenue equals total costs incurred and number of units sold; profit is not a bad word, but it is hard work.

11. What kind of financing will the company need, from where will it come, what is the type of financing—debt, equity, and/or grants.

12. How will the money that the company needs be paid back: stocks, warrants, loan payment schedules, and others.

13. How much money has been invested to date and where did it come from. Indicate monetary investment to date.

14. What potential innovation of the product/service will ensure long-term growth. Specifically identify what makes it difficult for competitors to enter.

15. Describe any unusual contracts or relationships that the company is or may become involved in. Include employee contracts, noncompete agreements, buy/sell agreements, off-shore relationships, and others.

The ultimate acid test is now to write one of your own.

NOTES

1. For more on this topic suggested readings are Sahar Hashemi and Bobby Hashemi, *Anyone Can Do It* (Chichester: Capstone Publishing, 2004); John W. Mullins, *The New Business Road Test* (London: FT Prentice Hall, 2003); Mike Southon and Chris West, *The Beermat Entrepreneur* (London: Pearson Prentice Hall Business, 2002); Caspian Woods, *From Acorns . . .* (London: Pearson Prentice Hall Business, 2004).

2. Peter F. Drucker, *The Essential Drucker* (New York: Harper Business, 2001), especially Chapter 3.

Four

Entrepreneurial Strategies: Defy Competition and Enter the Market

Closely connected with concept development is the choice of strategy that the entrepreneur can employ for bringing products and services to the market. The chosen strategy is in fact very much dependent on the business concept. In much of the business literature, and especially marketing literature, these strategies are known as *market penetration strategies*. While the marketing literature refers to new products and services, the same rationale can be applied when bringing a new venture to the market. But the entrepreneur conducts what could be regarded as double market entry, that is, bringing the firm to the market and then the product(s) or the service(s) the new venture offers. Both are equally challenging. The entrepreneur is faced with not only creating the firm and the product but also simultaneously controlling competition.

For many starting entrepreneurs, the task of handling competitors is new and many are quite unprepared. For one thing, the new firm threatens to reduce the competitor's share of the market and, depending on how big a threat this is, competitors will retaliate to defend and secure their own market and profit level. This in turn means that actions by competitors are aimed at keeping the new firm's profits down by keeping them either out of the market or taking back their market share at any cost.

A new firm certainly adds complexity to established industry dynamics. How big an impact the new entrant will have on industry dynamics depends on the particular products or services they offer. As most new firms are replicators, that is, they offer a service or a product which is already on the market, the effect will mainly be that of reducing profits. Survival will then be determined based on the carrying capacity of the industry.[1] However, in the case where the new entrant offers superior value and service, or a radical innovation, the new entrant may drive existing players out of business. A new player can even change the business ecosystem. One way of dealing with competition is to continuously innovate.[2]

Important for any entrepreneur is to understand that there is *always* competition in one way or the other, although many do declare there is no competition. One of the two things is true when such a claim is made: (1) one has not looked, or (2) there is no market. On the upside, competition tells the new firm that there is a need among people who are willing to pay to have it met. Michael E. Porter[3] describes the five competitive forces that shape industry competition in his classic book *Competitive Strategy*—highly recommendable for reading.

Founders of new companies must find a way to break through the defenses of the competition and enter the market. While the ideal method will vary by industry and by entrepreneur, finding the right way is essential for survival. Dealing with competition is one justification for the necessity to build a network.[4]

When entering the market there are a number of strategies for an entrepreneur to choose among three forms of innovation:[5] (1) product innovation, (2) process innovation, and (3) business concept innovation, all of which hinge on the original Schumpeterian rationale of entrepreneurship, that is, newness. However, there are also other approaches, such as sponsorship of a start-up, acquiring a business, or franchising. The last example is one which some would argue is not real entrepreneurship unless the entrepreneur creates a business concept which can be implemented as a franchise.

Each approach provides a unique set of strengths and weaknesses. We will describe each of them and show how each can be used in starting a new business regardless of the particular product or service you develop. In addition, the risks associated with each entry strategy will be presented.

PRODUCT INNOVATION—NEW PRODUCT OR SERVICE

Every item used in daily life began as a new product somewhere. Cars, televisions, dishwashers, paper towels, airlines, computers, and ketchup were all introduced to consumers at some point. The same can be said with services like dry cleaning, long-distance phone service, or massage therapy. Many entrepreneurs are constantly thinking of new products or services and bringing them to consumers. Needless to say, some succeed while many fail.

Products or services that succeed do so because they are solutions or answers to unmet customer needs, wants, or fears.[6] Moreover, the target market is willing to pay the price of the product or service in exchange for the benefits it provides. Because the product is new, the firm faces no direct competition;

that is, competition comes from substitutes or complementary products that mostly hold a mature position on the market. The challenge for anyone offering the new product is to ensure that customers make the switch; that is, the customer not only shows an interest or merely tries, but also adopts. Direct competition occurs when new competitors enter the market. The first entrant will enjoy the benefit of first mover, which gives them a beneficial learning curve and knowledge base. Any entrant behind the first will have to develop their own product and catch up with the pioneering company. There are occasions when the first mover advantage is a real competitive one but the second entrant is the one winning the game. This occurs if the technology or the product is not fully developed or the market is underdeveloped. That is, the second entrant can correct the mistakes of the first mover and acquire an advantage in the process. This has particularly been the case within information and communications technology (ICT), where the technology is under constant development, and consumer needs, wants, and fears are constantly changing.

However, developing a new product or service is not foolproof. Developing new products is mostly the most expensive way of entering a market. Knowing that most firms start off with little, if any, assets and constrained financial resources, this strategy is indeed risky for a new firm. An excellent example and perhaps an extreme one, but not rare and therefore justified here, of how difficult this strategy is to implement is provided by biotechnology firms. Small R&D based firms developing new drugs require up to fifteen years of product development before entering the market. This means that the firm has a negative cash flow for fifteen years. Very few companies have succeeded in their endeavor.

New enterprises that try to enter the market with a new product or service face the following risks:

1. The company may have design errors or defects.
2. Another company with stronger resources may follow the company's lead and push them out of the market.
3. The enterprise may not be able to persuade enough people to buy the new product fast enough or at a high enough price to make a profit.
4. The product or service may be appealing to too small of a market to be profitable.

New product and service development and implementation will be discussed in greater detail later.

PROCESS INNOVATION AND CONCEPT INNOVATION

An alternative to creating a brand new product category is to create a competing product in an existing category. Typically, the product is different enough to allow it to enter the marketplace. The newness here rests on either process or concept innovation. In general, product and process innovation share an important relationship, where product innovation is considered rapid and precedes process innovation, which is slower.[7] In process innovation, the product or the service as such already exists on the market. This is often referred to as parallel competition. For example, when the Southwest Airlines began operating they were not providing a new service, since air travel had been established long ago. However, their offer of inexpensive, short-distance flights was unique enough to allow the airline to succeed and flourish. Southwest Airlines provided added value at a competitive price. Another example is Starbucks. Americans had for years been drinking coffee, but Starbucks changed the way coffee was sold to consumers and essentially relaunched coffee on the American market. Starbucks has since established itself in many countries worldwide, but not in France or Italy, as espresso coffee is drunk from small cups not 8-ounce cups!

Often, individuals who start companies in existing industries have worked in those industries before, and are using their prior knowledge and expertise to create a new offering, an improved concept.

Parallel competition is fierce. While new entrants may be slightly different, they often do not have enough differentiation to attract a new market. Hence all competitors—old and new—are fighting for the same customers. Frequently, parallel competition leads to competition on price, which reduces margins and is detrimental to all players, in particular to new entrants. New entrants face the challenge of competing with larger competitors who may have greater economies of scale and flexibility in pricing.

There are a number of factors driving process and concept innovation. One refers to location, that is, the possibility of transferring a product or service to a new location. As such, this does not necessarily involve an innovative act, but can do so. It is the possibility that a venture could potentially expand to multiple locations that has to be recognized by the entrepreneur. This was clearly the case of Luciano Benetton, the women's wear retailer. Another one is recognizing an approaching critical supply shortage when consumer demand grows. Entrepreneurs, who recognize this phenomenon early and can provide additional supply, can establish themselves in the market by filling unmet levels of demand. Finally, it is the ability to capitalize on unused resources. When there is an overcapacity, there is an opportunity to use the excess resources for an alternate purpose. For example, entrepreneurs have found a way to use excess grain or sugar to produce ethanol, a gasoline substitute. How successful a substitute ethanol is in reality remains to be seen. Right now it certainly is an attractive possibility.

The primary risks of process or concept innovation are

1. The start-up may be unable to compete with established competitors in pricing, customer service, product quality, and so on.
2. Existing competitors may develop a new product or alter existing ones to compete against the new entrant's unique attributes.
3. New companies may underestimate the amount of loyalty customers have to the existing competitors or the amount of resources necessary to build credibility and trial.
4. In transferring a product to a new location, entrepreneurs must be about to recruit the capital and staff for the new site. They run the risk of not finding enough money and staff to start or maintain the operation.
5. Supply shortages will eventually go away. Therefore, entrepreneurs who choose this form of entry must be prepared for extreme competitive pressure when the shortage ends.
6. Unused resources may look appealing. However, the entrepreneur runs the risk that the new product or the use of the resource will be unwanted by consumers.

STRATEGIC ALLIANCE OR PARTNERING

Entrepreneurs who prefer a safer way to enter the market may search for a sponsor or a strategic alliance or partner. The "sponsor" in this case is someone willing to help the entrepreneur start his or her enterprise in some manner. The main types of alliances are

- Customer Alliances—A potential customer who is eager to obtain the product or service that the new venture would produce may be willing to partner with the entrepreneur in the endeavor. This comes in the form of a large purchase order, a contract to purchase over a certain amount of time, or a cash advance on future purchases.
- Supplier Alliances—A supplier may want to see more ventures formed that use the product or service they offer. As a result, they may be willing to advance inventory or labor as a way of easing the firm's formation.
- Investor Alliances—Often someone who thinks the venture will become highly successful will provide a cash advance to the business and become an investor. Typically, investors make these contributions to make a profit. However, they may also like the entrepreneur or feel the venture is a good cause to support. Some might consider family "investor sponsors."

In order to secure sponsorships or alliances, entrepreneurs must have a venture or business opportunity that potential sponsors consider credible and likely to succeed. Most accomplish this by showing a track record of success or proving that they possess the skills critical for creating and managing the endeavor.

Sponsorship approaches or strategic alliances carry the following risks:

1. Entrepreneurs can lose credibility if their venture fails, and the sponsors lose what they invested or provided to the business. This can make it more difficult to secure sponsorship for future ventures.
2. Sponsors can feel they have a certain amount of control over the venture.
3. Sponsors may pressure the entrepreneur to act according to their own goals and objectives and not for the good of the venture.

ACQUISITION

Next, there is the possibility of acquisition of an existing business. At first this may not seem very entrepreneurial, but we have a number of colleagues who use this approach religiously because of the often underutilized or undervalued assets in an existing business. This option is appealing because it tremendously simplifies the process of starting a business, although one has the culture of an established firm not desirable. The operations are already in place, the customers already exist, and the place in the market has already been established. Additionally, the cash flow from the business should provide a fairly clear picture of what the financial needs are and what the profit potential is. Acquiring a business circumvents the negative cash flow and the struggling period that all start-up organizations go through. Finally, by purchasing a business, one can avoid, for a period of time, the need for two things: expertise and capital.

Expertise should be present in an existing enterprise in the employees of the existing business. If the expertise lies in the owner who is selling the business, then the entrepreneur can negotiate the exchange of his or her knowledge through an agreement to advise, train, or educate the new owner. As a result, many entrepreneurs who purchase a growing concern may have no experience in that field, whereas in a start-up the entrepreneur must be the expert. The need for capital is often avoided by having the selling owner help with the financing through leveraging the buyout. The entrepreneur purchasing the company can often borrow against the assets of the company to provide a down payment to the seller and some working capital to continue operations. The buyer then pays the rest off to the seller over time from the earnings of the operation. This approach requires the support of competent legal advice, and it is necessary to fully understand the valuation of the firm. Most sellers overvalue their business unless they are near bankruptcy. Acquiring a bankrupt business and turning it around is not recommended for any starting entrepreneur as a way of becoming an entrepreneur.

Acquiring firms is clearly not risk-free. Risks that the entrepreneur must consider when thinking of purchasing a business are in three primary areas. These involve finding the right business to purchase, how its value is established, and how favorable terms for the purchase are negotiated. Needless to say, this calls for some experience, which is why legal and financial advice is recommended.

FRANCHISE

One way of starting a firm is to purchase a franchise. Franchise is a contract that allows an entrepreneur to open a branch of an existing business with, hopefully, a proven business concept. That is, somebody else has created the concept, and the entrepreneur just buys the right to use the same concept. Many fast-food restaurant chains in the United States provide good examples, say McDonald's, Taco Bell, and Subways. Other areas where franchising is common are gas stations, car dealers, and many retail stores.

Typically, a franchise agreement grants the entrepreneur the right to use the business's brand name and logo, to sell its products, and to use its methods of production. In addition, the existing company, also called the franchisor, may provide training, accounting, financing, and marketing. The entrepreneur, or franchise, is granted the right to operate in a certain geographic area so that he/she does not compete with other franchisees. In exchange for these rights, the franchisee must make a cash payment for the franchise and often certain royalties after that. The entrepreneur will usually supply the capital to equip and operate the franchise.

Many entrepreneurs who purchase franchises have no experience in that field but they manage because of the support from the franchisor. This is one way of learning to become an entrepreneur and a very attractive way to enter a new industry. Established firms use franchising to expand their business quickly with minimal investment. On the other hand, some think that franchising is not "real" entrepreneurship. A colleague once said, "Frankly, I am not a great fan of buying a franchise, but I am a fan of those who create concepts that can be franchised."

The risk of purchasing a franchise include the following:

1. The franchisor may fail to be completely honest about the likely success of the franchise or the amount of support the franchisee will receive.
2. The franchisee may have too little start-up capital to survive until break-even.

3. The franchisee might have to open several outlets to gain substantial profits that may be beyond their available capital.

4. Consumer trends may move away from the franchisor's business and they may be slow to respond, leaving the franchisee with sinking sales.

NOTES

1. Howard E. Aldrich, *Organizations Evolving* (London: Sage Publications, 1999).

2. Henry W. Chesbrough, *Open Innovation: The New Imperative for Creating and Profiting from Technology* (Boston, MA: Harvard Business School Press, 2003); Clayton M. Christensen, Scott D. Anthony, and Erik A. Roth, *Seeing What's Next: Using Theories of Innovations to Predict Industry Change* (Boston, MA: Harvard Business School Press, 2004); W. Chan Kim and Reneé Mauborgne, *Blue Ocean Strategy: How to Create Uncontested Market Space and Make Competition Irrelevant* (Boston, MA: Harvard Business School Press, 2005); Geoffrey A. Moore, *Dealing with Darwin: How Great Companies Innovate at Every Phase of Their Evolution* (New York: Portfolio, 2005); James F. Moore, *The Death of Competition: Leadership Strategy in the Age of Business Ecosystems* (Hoboken, NJ: John Wiley & Sons, 1996); James M. Utterback, *Mastering the Dynamics of Innovation* (Boston, MA: Harvard Business School Press, 1996); see also Chapter 2 in this book.

3. Michael E. Porter, *Competitive Strategy* (New York: The Free Press, 1980).

4. Ibid.

5. Gary Hamel, *Leading the Revolution* (Boston, MA: Harvard Business School Press, 2000).

6. Porter, *Competitive Strategy*; see also Chapter 3 in this book.

7. James M. Utterback, *Mastering the Dynamics of Innovation* (Boston, MA: Harvard Business School Press, 1996).

Five

Creating New Products and Services

If innovation is one of the defining factors for being an entrepreneur, then the development of viable new products and services are critical behaviors that an entrepreneur needs to master. Creating new products and services or continuously improving existing ones is a key to sustaining competitive ability. Today, this means adopting a customer-oriented approach, that is, listening to customer needs, wants, and fears. The days when technology would sell by itself—what sometimes is referred to as "build it, they will come" strategy to new products or services—have outlived themselves a long time ago, and this is not an effective strategy.[1] In this chapter we discuss ways for an entrepreneur to develop new products and services. This process is closely related to business concept development and even idea generation. In fact, there are those who will argue that these activities are inherently all the same. It is possible to partially agree with that claim, but for pedagogic purposes they are here kept apart. This chapter will discuss why new product and service ideas fail or succeed, and why early market research can help produce better products and services on which to base a new venture.

While innovation appears to define an entrepreneur, especially the Schumpeterian entrepreneur, product innovation defines a manufacturer. Eric von Hippel expands our understanding of innovation by speaking of functional sources innovation, and suddenly we understand that innovators are not just entrepreneurs or manufacturers. In fact, it reveals to us a range of innovators who are available to both manufacturers and entrepreneurs. Thus, we may start with deriving the benefit from a specific innovation, be it a product, service, process, or business concept. If they benefit from using, they are users. If they benefit from producing, they are manufacturers. They can also be suppliers. And, they can also be entrepreneurs![2]

The most common procedure is the *stage-gate model* of product development. This model can reduce the time and costs associated with failed products and increase the probability of success.[3] This is important because it is estimated that 80 percent of new products and services fail.

If there is ever a place where the entrepreneur needs interdisciplinary teams from technology, to design, to marketing, to human factors, it is in the area of new product and service development. The process of creating something new requires being comfortable with ambiguity, the willingness to do the difficult work of transforming ideas into real physical products and deliverable service. To have a new product or service you need to assure that your product or service is

- Superior
- Well researched
- Market-driven
- Well launched
- Well designed
- Has an attractive market
- Well supported

In other words, the key success factor is to have a well-defined product or service concept prior to development, a carefully defined and assessed target market, thoroughly developed product requirements and benefits, technical and marketing synergy, a high quality of execution, and market attractiveness.[4]

The real test for any good product or service development is how to avoid creating a *dud*. Examples of *duds* that have made their ways into history are Boo.com, Pets.com, eToys, Motorola's Iridium, and Philips' CD-I video-music-game systems. What all these have in common is that millions, if not billions, of dollars were spent on their development. All were failures. But why do most new products fail? Common reasons for failure are (1) overestimated market, (2) underestimated competition, (3) poor design, (4) poor positioning, advertising, or pricing, (5) failure to recognize flaws in a favorite idea, and (6) insufficient cost control.

Product development is always a challenging process but especially so when developing a technology-based product or service. In previous chapters we saw that potential sources of ideas to good products are potential lead users, strategic partners within the firm (if it already exists), from customer complaints, competitors, or from product-generating firms. Below are examples of ideas that came from resolving an inconvenience:

1. When people drop their cell phone it breaks and ceases to function. Obviously, both Nokia and Samsung had observed this and have provided sturdier design of their cell phones.

2. The idea for a paper cell phone came from a user frustrated over a lost phone call. The person wanted to throw the phone away but could not because of the cost of the phone.

The latter idea alters the view that cell phones should be more rugged, which in turn is the basis for the former line of reasoning. Hence, opportunity recognition for a new product quite often hinges on the unexpected, the incongruent, the unusual; or changes in industry, market structure, or demographic shifts; or changes in customers' perception or moods; or as the result of new knowledge.

In general, there are four economic conditions that successful ideas appear to share. These are based on systematic and rational thought and defeat the common misunderstanding that innovative ideas and new business creation are random processes, where luck and serendipity are key elements. These conditions are

- Buyer Utility
- Strategic Pricing
- Business Model
- Adoption Hurdles

Buyer utility means that there is a compelling reason for a customer to buy a new product or service. Such reasons come from the ability of the product or service to address the needs, wants, and fears of customers. Moreover, it is important to remember that utility and technological advance are not the same. The concept of *strategic pricing* refers to the ability to price the new product or service to attract the masses of buyers. *Business model* connects back to the discussion in the prior chapter of strategic alternatives (purchase, acquisition, and so on) on how you are going to profitably deliver the new product or service idea. *Adoption hurdles* refer to the reasons an idea may not be accepted by customers, employees, partners, or society.

An example that ties these four concepts together and shows the importance of all four issues is provided by the technology marvel by Phillips: the CD-I. The CD-I has often been described as a masterpiece of engineering with diverse functions. Slightly exaggerating, the CD-I was considered to be theoretically capable of doing almost anything, but in reality it could do very little. Usability and user friendliness for nonengineers was minimal, and the product did not invite the user the slightest bit as it lacked attractive software titles. It became a multimillion-dollar failure. This product failed because people do not buy a mediocre product that does lots of things "so-so." It failed also because entertainment electronics will not succeed without the software side and there was no incentive for the media companies to produce that software. This is most obvious with the cast of VHS over Sony BETA.[5] VHS won the war for customers not only because of its technology, but also because it provided a *value proposition* for the pornographic industry of a cheap vehicle to sell their product to be used by adults in the privacy of their own homes.

Experience has shown, although contrary to what is often claimed in public, that the most important part of a product is not necessarily its technology. Buyer utility is the most important driver of success. Buyer utility in turn is dependent on six factors: customer productivity, simplicity, convenience, risk mitigation, fun and image, and environmental friendliness. This can be summarized into two words: *usability* and *user-friendliness*.[6] We will examine each of these with examples.

Customer productivity attempts to identify the biggest constrains of customer productivity. The key to a successful product is whether the innovative product or service eliminates the constraint. A simple example is the Hoover vacuum cleaner. Earlier women beat rugs with sticks or paddles to clean them; with the invention of the Hoover vacuum cleaner it became quicker and easier to clean rugs; that is, it significantly increased customer productivity (and buyer utility). There clearly was a compelling reason for anyone to buy the product. The product also addressed *simplicity*. Thus, a fundamental question is whether the product or the service significantly simplifies a previous activity. A good example is Intuit's Quicken software. Not only did it eliminate accounting jargon from personal financial accounting but with its business version it also made bookkeeping easier and reduced the number of accounting bills. Moreover, both Hoover and Quicken addressed another key feature: *convenience*. Thinking of inconveniences, such as when spotting a poor service or a product with a complex user interface, can help one discover a viable business. A product should significantly reduce the inconvenience.

The fourth factor is *risk mitigation*, which is not an easy one to grasp. Quicken software reduces the risk of fraud. For Hoover, it could be reducing the risk of having an untidy room. Risk reduction addresses an inherent part of human nature: *fear*. How can a product reduce fear; or, put another way, how can it address the greatest uncertainties buyers face? It is therefore necessary to show that a product or service can eliminate these risks or reduce the fear. Paradoxically, there are unintended consequences for most things, and, especially in the United States, it is necessary to anticipate the potential new risks a product or service can cause. An example of risk mitigation is provided by the energy firm Enron, whose commodity swaps and futures contracts stripped the volatility out of gas and electric prices. The unintended consequence was that it ended up hurting many customers through fraud. The concept was sound, the firm and its leadership were not. A good concept can fail because of the unethical (and certainly illegal) behaviors of management.

It often comes as a surprise that *fun* and *image* are central to the success of a product or service. Disney certainly understood the necessity of fun, and LVMH (Motet Hennessy Louis Vuitton) certainly understood that it is possible to run a profitable business by selling products nobody needs, but *Oh SO desires!*[7] The entire luxury business is built on *un-necessities*, that few really need, but very many yearn and desire for. Hence it is relevant to consider whether a product or a service is capable of generating positive emotion or cachet to the buyer. Positive emotion is not luxury, but is nice. A product capable of radiating a positive image about its owner or user has a source of a *compelling reason to buy*. For example, Starbucks' chic coffee bars are much more than a place to buy a hot drink. It is clearly an affordable indulgence.

Finally, *environmental friendliness* is a feature that in today's global business cannot be ignored anymore. In northern Europe this has been an issue for almost three decades. Ignoring this factor is an almost certain recipe for market failure. Hence, while developing a product or service it is necessary to ask what causes the greatest harm to the environment. Does the product or service reduce or eliminate this? One example is provided by Phillips' Alto light bulb, which uses less mercury than earlier designs. This means eliminating the costs of special dumping sites in Europe. Another example is toilet paper or paper made from recycled newspapers.

WINNING WAY FOR NEW PRODUCT AND SERVICE DEVELOPMENT

It sounds simple to tell somebody to work only on the right projects when developing a new product or service. The difficult thing is to learn to spend the necessary time on project selection and being willing to build tough Go/Kill decision points. Most entrepreneurs or innovators find it very hard to seriously question their own projects (babies) and to actually arrive at a decision that means abandoning the idea or killing the project. However, it is necessary to do so. Unfortunately, many projects get terminated way too late and thereby manage to kill the entire venture as the cash reserves get dried out. Many of the questions in the checklists provided throughout the book offer the kind of tough questions an entrepreneur has to ask. Too many *no* or *no idea* answers means *Please seriously consider terminating!*

Even when it seems that the right project has been chosen, more questions need to be asked during the development process, and at anytime the result may be *terminate!* You find the right ideas by killing the bad ones. These questions are aimed at doing the specific project right. One of the most common ways to win and bring new products or services to market quickly and effectively is to use the stage-gate process.[8] It has been estimated that over 68 percent of US product developers use some form of a stage-gate process. *A stage-gate process is a conceptual and operational road map for managing the new product or service process to improve effectiveness and efficiency.*

OVERVIEW OF THE STAGE-GATE PROCESS

The stage-gate process divides the product or service development process into a predetermined set of stages. This provides a structure to the creative process and serves to improve the decision-making process. Each stage consists of a set of prescribed, cross-functional, and parallel activities, and each gate precedes each stage and serves as the quality control point and the Go/Kill checkpoint. The secret is to do the right project in the right way!

An extreme but a very visual example of a stage-gate model is the drug development model with different stages (a rough model is shown in Figures 5.1 and 5.2). The arrows in Figure 5.1 show that a project can be terminated at any point of time. In the case of drug development, regulatory requirements function as stage gates. If a drug candidate fails a clinical test—or a preclinical test—it has to be terminated as it will never be approved by, for example, the Food and Drug Administration. A drug cannot be sold without this approval.

FIGURE 5.1

A Stage-gate Model, a Rough Model of Drug Development

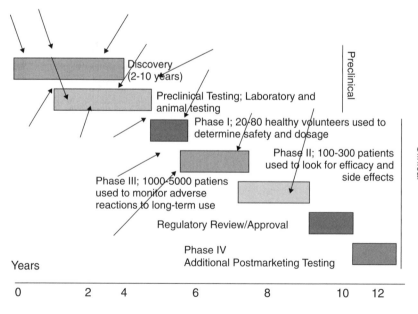

FIGURE 5.2
A Detailed Stage-gate of Drug Development

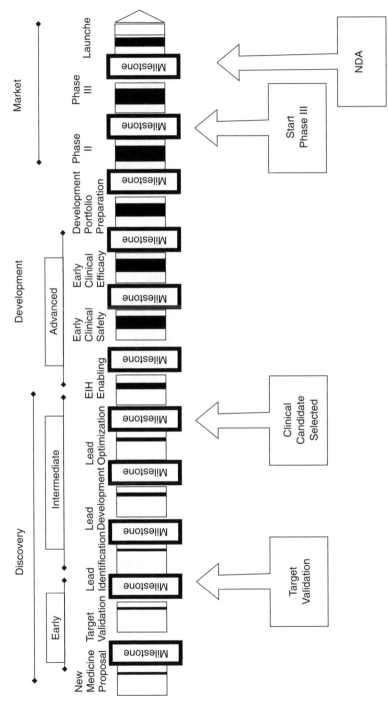

A stage-gate model typically consists of five stages. Sometimes, as in Figures 5.1 and 5.2 there are more, and in fact within each phase there are numerous stages (but this is an extreme example). In its simplicity the five stages are the following:

Stage 1—Initial investigation of the project.

Stage 2—Detailed investigation of the project. At this stage a business case of the project should be created (define product, business justification, and detailed plan of action for the next stages).

Stage 3—Advanced design and development. It is important to define manufacturing and operating process, marketing launch strategy, and test plans for next stage.

Stage 4—Testing and validation. The product is carefully verified and plans for marketing and production are made.

Stage 5—Launch and full commercialization, production, marketing, and selling.

Each stage costs more than the preceding one, so stages are based on incremental commitment. Each stage aims at reducing uncertainties, although the expenditures of each stage increase (reducing risk is expensive!). Each stage has to be seen as a detailed list of activities and deliverables that resembles a funnel rather than a tunnel.[9] There are Go/Kill decisions and prioritization points, which serve as quality control checkpoints (see Figure 5.2). Remember that resource commitments should be determined by "gatekeepers," some of whom may be within the organization and some external partners, advisors, and investors. Effective gates are central to the success of the stage-gate process. It is vital to know when to cut one's losses so that the future is not jeopardized. In Figure 5.2 the concept of *milestones* is introduced, and here it visualizes the reality of drug development companies. Each milestone may be a point of agreement with a partner, which means payment to the developer at each point. Failing to reach a milestone may at worst allow the partner to break the partnership, or sometimes that point may be subject to costs of delay.

To use the stage-gate process requires sufficient cross-functional teams and people willing to support each other, and above all it requires an effective gate-keeping group or individual. For larger organizations it often means senior managers with resource allocation authority at later gates.

However, the stage-gate process can be limited by slow decision making, as it needs resources and the so-called standing gate-keeping groups for different projects to allocate resources effectively. A stage-gate process may be difficult for a start-up firm to afford, but the benefits outweigh the costs and limitations. Next, we will review two stages that to our minds seem the most challenging ones in product and service development: preliminary investigation, and advanced development or prototyping.

PRELIMINARY INVESTIGATION

For some reason this appears to be the stage that is often omitted by many innovators and entrepreneurs. At this stage preliminary market assessments as well as technical and business assessments are made. The key word here is *preliminary*. This means that too much time should not be spent if there are early indications that the idea is not particularly good.

A preliminary market assessment includes

- Market existence and stage
- Market size, growth, and potential
- Market segments
- Consumer interest
- Competition

This is essentially desk research and the Internet is extremely instrumental, provided one knows how to search the Internet. Surprisingly, many often fail to check the one source that changes very little and that is available at a very high level of detail in almost any country—demographic data. In the United States this is provided by US Census; in Finland the source would be Statistics Finland. Of course, there are market reports available for purchase, but they are expensive, and even if the report has just been released, the data in the report may be three or four years old. The Internet often provides much more current information—and often for free. It is suggested you check out the demographic data available at http://www.census.gov/ and www.statistics.fi and also at http://cyberatlas.internet.com/big_picture/ stats_toolbox/article/0,,6081_156101,00.html.

A preliminary technical assessment explores proposed technical solutions, including rough technical and performance criteria. This process involves the review of competitive solutions, and at this stage it is necessary to conduct a patent search. Patent data is public information and again available online (http://www.uspto.gov/). This stage also includes a technical and potentially legal risk assessment.

A preliminary business assessment estimates the business risks associated with this product or service. This is not limited to legal risks alone, but also includes less tangible issues like ethical risks. As part of this a financial case for the product/service should be created, including payback period for investment and very rough sales, costs, and investment figures.

ADVANCED DEVELOPMENT: PROTOTYPING, PARTNERING, AND PRICING

This stage of the product-service development process is one that begins to blend into the business plan development process. It includes prototyping of the product or service, the development of needed partnerships and alliances, and pricing. Pricing is perhaps the part of this process that most closely impacts the development of a viable business plan and the marketing plan for the product based on earlier market analysis.

PROTOTYPING

Prototyping is important regardless of whether the product is a new food dish, software system, or silicon chips. Prototypes reduce uncertainty through four basic purposes:

- Learning: serves as a proof-of-concept model.
- Communication: demonstrates the product or service for feedback, for example, 3D physical or computerized models.
- Integration: combines subsystems into system model.
- Milestones to push the process forward (Figure 5.2).

There are multiple types of prototypes, although the two types most people are familiar with are physical and analytical prototypes. Physical prototypes are tangible approximations of the product. They may exhibit unmodeled behaviors and some behaviors may be an artifact of the approximation. A physical prototype is often best for communication. Analytical prototypes are usually mathematical models of the product. They can only exhibit behavior arising from explicitly modeled phenomena. However, some behaviors are not always anticipated, as bridge, building, and airplane builders have learned the hard way. Some of the behaviors may be an artifact of the analytical method, but the big advantage is that analytical approaches can allow more experimental freedom than physical models. Above all, it is important to realize that one prototype is seldom enough. It is important to understand that virtually every industry has its own prototyping phases and processes (as shown in Figures 5.1 and 5.2 with drug development).

Often used methods for prototyping are layers based on CAD (Computer Aided Design) models, SLA (Stereo Lithography Apparatus), SLS (Selective Laser Sintering), 3D Printing, LOM (Laminated Object Manufacturing), CNC (Computer Numerically Controlled) machining, rubber molding and urethane casting, and models made of materials like wood, foam, plastics, paper, and others. It is necessary to understand that prototypes are critical to receiving funding and ultimate success.

PARTNERSHIPS AND ALLIANCES IN PRODUCT DEVELOPMENT

Partnerships and alliances have long been common in marketing and distribution. Over the years, new product developments in industries as diverse as wines and pharmaceuticals are increasingly the result of strategic partnerships and alliances. Few industries conduct product development en solo today. Not even in the pharmaceutical industry (Figures 5.1 and 5.2) is the fully integrated product development model the prevailing one any more. The fully integrated model means that the entire development process is carried out in-house. Still, two decades ago, it was considered that R&D had to be conducted in-house as it was the secret sauce to success. Today, every stage can be the basis for a business (each arrow in Figure 5.1 could point at a business). And this is true in most industries. Hence, partnerships and alliances are the rules rather than the exceptions to product development.

Partnerships can help you produce prototypes at an accelerated rate. For example, many new firms in Silicon Valley have sped up the formation of an entire product infrastructure within specific target market segments by using alliances for distribution of vital components and their installations. Networking is key in partnering (see Chapter 2 of this book).

PRICING

Some may argue that pricing is not an issue for product development, but we think it is very important to consider price, cost, and value as part of the product development process.

First and foremost, price should be based on value, not cost. The price has to cover the costs, but above all reflect the perceived value of the product or service. If the product adds value, by ultimately providing the customer with a compelling reason to buy, the price will not be the most decisive criterion leading up to the choice to buy. There are numerous examples of expensive products adding very little value and therein not justifying the high price. The customer is not attracted and the product fails to recoup the costs. Similarly, there are many examples of the misconception that a low price will make any product an easy sell. A product with significant added value with a low price is potentially only leaving a lot of "money on the table." It is important to understand that it is always easier to drop a price than to raise it. Ask any supplier to Wal-Mart if they know that lesson. Hence it is important to understand what role the price plays in terms of the customers' decision-making

criteria. Is it the most important, or somewhat important, or not at all important? Once it is understood what role price has, it is possible to choose a
pricing strategy.

FINANCIAL CONSIDERATIONS OF NEW PRODUCTS AND SERVICES

At every stage of the process of building a new product or service it is necessary to make financial and time estimates. At each stage the quality of this
information will improve. Critical to gatekeepers are issues around payback
and break-even times. It is important here to think of time as money. The
following should be assessed early:

- Cycle time: Time from product initiation to market launch.
- Payback period: Time from launch to full recovery of initial expenditures.
- Break-even time: Time from product initiation to when all expenditures are
  recovered.

There are various methods that can be used to look at the quality of the
financial investment. Two key measures of financial investment are (1) net
present value (NPV), where cash flows are discounted to present values using
a discount rate (minimum acceptable return), and (2) internal rate of return
(IRR), where the discount rate is such that the NPV = 0.

It is necessary to look at the financial implications of any new product
or service being developed. It is even more important with most technology
products because in the next stage even more money and time are committed.
The immediate questions that require considerations with financial implications are

- Is the market attractive?
- Does it fit with the strategy of the new venture?
- Is it technically feasible?
- Are there any killer variables?
- What is the minimum acceptable probability of success?
- How could the probability be improved?

EXERCISES

The Elevator Pitch Exercise: An Encore

While most entrepreneurs and investors think of doing elevator pitches as
part of getting investors once you have a business plan, it is highly critical to

get people involved in the development of the proposed new product and service. If it is possible to briefly describe the product or service idea to another in nontechnical ways or without industrial jargon, it is a way of focusing on what the product or service really ought to be. The idea here is to sell an idea to others. Can the idea be explained in three minutes? This is the elevator pitch encore, but this time the product is essentially positioned. It is required to answer the following questions in an engaging way. Fill in the sentences!

Our new product is
   For (target customer segment),
   who are dissatisfied with (the current market alternatives).
Our product is a (new product category),
   which provides (key problem-solving capability),
   unlike (the product alternatives), and
   we have assembled (key whole product features for your specific application).

A Product Development Exercise

This exercise is for a team, with preferably at least four persons, creating a new product or service. One acts as the "facilitator" and another as "note taker." There are some rules to this exercise: no criticism or discussion of the value of one idea over another is allowed. Everyone gets a turn to present their ideas. Here are the steps:

- Step 1 (10 minutes): Everyone describes a product or activity that is a *pain*.
- Step 2 (5 minutes): Vote on the top 2 *pains*.
- Step 3 (15 minutes): Brainstorm solutions to each of those *pains*.
- Step 4 (up to a day): Assign ideas to owners and ask them to *flesh out the ideas*.
- Step 5: Keep all ideas for a formal review later.

The point is to keep ideas for new products or services coming. This can be an old technology for other new uses.

- Be willing to modify, adapt, or magnify (bigger, stronger, higher) the ideas generated.
- Consider substitutes for current products or services (what else can be used, or who else can provide).
- Rearrange, reverse, or combine existing services.

NOTES

1. Peter F. Drucker, *The Essential Drucker* (New York: Harper Business, 2001); Theodor Levitt, "Marketing Myopia," *Harvard Business Review* 53 (1975): 12.

2. Henry W. Chesbrough, *Open Innovation: The New Imperative for Creating and Profiting from Technology* (Boston, MA: Harvard Business School Press, 2003); Gary Hamel, *Leading the Revolution* (Boston, MA: Harvard Business School Press, 2000); Eric von Hippel, *Sources of Innovation* (New York: Oxford University Press, 1988); James M. Utterback, *Mastering the Dynamics of Innovation* (Boston, MA: Harvard Business School Press, 1996).

3. Robert G. Cooper, *Winning at New Products* (Reading, MA: Addison-Wesley Publishing, 1986); Vijay K. Jolly, *Commercializing New Technologies* (Boston, MA: Harvard Business School Press, 1997).

4. Kathleen R. Allen, *Bringing New Technology to Market* (New York: Prentice Hall, 2002).

5. Michael A. Cusumano, Yiorgos Mylonadis, and Richard S. Rosenbloom, "Strategic Maneuvering and Mass-Market Dynamics: The Triumph of VHS over Beta," in *Managing Strategic Innovation and Change*, eds. Michael L. Tushman and Philip Anderson (New York: Oxford University Press, 1997): 75–98.

6. Donald A. Norman, *The Design of Everyday Things* (Cambridge, MA: MIT Press, 1998).

7. Suzy Wetlaufer, "The Perfect Paradox of Star Brands," *Harvard Business Review* 79 (2001): 116–123.

8. Jolly, *Commercializing New Technologies*; Chesbrough, *Open Innovation: The New Imperative*.

9. Chesbrough, *Open Innovation: The New Imperative*.

PART III

THE EXTERNAL ENVIRONMENT AND COMPETITIVE LANDSCAPE

Six

Building a Strategy: Understand the Industry and Competition

THE CONCEPT OF STRATEGY—A BRIEF REVIEW

Developing effective strategies to start and grow an entrepreneurial firm is not rocket science, but a careful blend of science, art, and intuition cooked over the flame of experience. The concept of strategy is both implicitly and explicitly very old. The roots of the implicit dimension of strategy date back to the Chinese warlord Sun Tzu, approximately 400 BC, or a somewhat newer version of strategic thinking that concerned the management of an Italian principality during the Middle Ages. Explicitly, the concept of strategy goes back to 510 BC when Kleistenes in Athens created ten tribal divisions with a *strategos*, or a strategist, as the head of each division. These ten strategists formed the Athenian war council, which also controlled nonmilitary politics.[1]

The concept of strategy entered the business field en masse much later, in the 1960s. The reference to military connotations still remains there and has also been made although Andrews firmly argues that corporate strategy is something more.[2] Hence strategy in business is primarily not about war, although the entire marketing strategy vocabulary surely makes you believe it is about war: "[W]e *launch* marketing campaigns based on *strategies* that *target* markets; we *bombard* people with messages in order to *penetrate* markets. . . . Business-as-usual is in constant state of war with the market, with the Marketing department manning the front lines."[3]

Closely related to strategy has always been leadership, either in that form or in terms of management. In other words, strategy is something in someone's head or on paper in someone's hands when taking leading action (either as a general or general manager). An ancient Athenian scholar, Xenophon, argued that a leader should possess certain characteristics in order to become an excellent strategist (qualities that are still generally regarded as good)[4]. A leader should be ingenious, energetic, careful, full of stamina and presence of mind, loving and tough, straightforward and crafty, alert and deceptive, ready to gamble everything and wishing to have everything, generous and greedy, and trusting and yet suspicious.

Needless to say, history can portray quite a few examples of leadership, which are sometimes due to totally different qualities and where the methods of leadership have been very brutal and the lives of subordinates most apprehensive. For example, Petronius Arbiter, who served under Nero, stated in Satyricon: "It is not much use depending upon calculation when Fate has methods of her own."[5] Somewhat like the executive officers at Enron, Fate was another expression for "the Boss," which of course was Nero himself. Nero, as we know, was so powerful that it was not thought proper to mention him by name. We also know of his methods; the coliseum, the monument to killing, still exists in the heart of Rome.

Sometime in the 1960s, the concept of strategy entered the business leadership arena and gained stunning dominance. Näsi and Aunela concluded, "Hardly any other business concept has during the past decades become such a conceptual commodity. What other field within business leadership can portray as many textbooks, courses, consultancy firms or top management meetings than that of strategy?"[6] This popularity shows no sign of decline. However, there is a downside to this high esteem. With the vast numbers of scholars and practitioners, there has come fragmentation of the field most visible in the numerous schools of thought. For example, Näsi first presented six schools of thought and then, five years later, said ten. Mintzberg and Karlöf also counted to ten but with slightly different schools of thought. Gilbert and his colleagues specified six schools, Chaffe claimed three, and Johnson and Scholes concluded there were six. Then Mintzberg and his colleagues made the final call at ten unique schools of strategic thinking.[7] Regardless of what the proper number is, in all these schools we can find concepts and conceptual frameworks that are popular, important, and thus accepted as viable in practice by practicing entrepreneurs. What is more important, they are proof that schools of thought are products of thought and experience. In other words, strategy making and strategic management are cognitive processes aimed at ultimately taking action.

One can be easily led to believe that strategy and strategic management are merely dealing with operations and therefore are only action oriented.[8] However, strategy and strategic management are as much a result of cognition, as concluded by Gilbert and his colleagues:[9] "[T]he concept of strategy is the most important concept an executive needs for *understanding* and *contributing* to the success of a business." (Italics added.)

The strategy literature reveals that strategy can conceptually be viewed very differently. For example, six perspectives can exist separately or jointly:[10]

1. Strategy is an integrated decision-making model of the firm. It includes the understanding that strategy making is explicit and deliberate. As time flows, the decision-making model—the logic of the company—is sharpened, which requires an understanding of the roots of the company.
2. Strategy enforces the long-term mission of the firm.
3. Strategy determines the competitive scope of the firm.
4. Strategy is the operationalization of the SWOT analysis.
5. Strategy provides a system of structures for corporate, strategic business unit (SBU), and functional leadership.
6. Strategy provides an interactive model between the firm and its shareholders and stakeholders.

Depending on what role strategy has had within the organization, together with a continuous pursuit of operational excellence as means of competition, we have seen a flood of management techniques and tools presented to the ever more frustrated managers.[11] Words like portfolio planning, agenda, benchmarking, outsourcing, lean and agile management, total quality management, business process reengineering, competence-based competition, Malcolm Baldrige Award, quick ratios, customer-relationship management, SBU-thinking, key or critical success factors, fortify-and-defend strategies, joint ventures, strategic alliances, networking, and balanced scorecard (these are just a few examples, there are many more) are all very familiar concepts within large corporations. For entrepreneurs, these concepts can seem daunting. This is not to say that the techniques are irrelevant, but a starting entrepreneur may not desperately need all of these in the beginning. All these have at some point been introduced in a very sincere attempt to translate strategy into action, to somehow improve the logic of strategy, and to provide means of measuring that action. On the other hand, with a few exceptions, these tools are *how-to* tools designed to do differently what is already done; that is, many of them contribute to operational excellence and fail to address the equally important question *what-to*-do. As pointed out by Porter, operational excellence is not a sufficient basis for creating a sustainable competitive advantage because these techniques and tools are available to anyone ready to deploy them. That is, a strategy should be unique if it is to enable creation of a sustainable competitive advantage. Hence, these managerial techniques and tools, when freely available, are not sources of a sustainable competitive advantage. They require something else to go along with them, and that is strategic positioning.[12] Strategic positioning requires a comprehensive managerial understanding of the business the entrepreneur is trying to develop and launch.[13]

The most common way to look at strategy is as a process of planning aiming at providing a systematic approach to express where the firm ought to be in the future and what it ought to do to achieve a set of goals. The planning perspective evolved in the 1960s and 1970s, and quickly became widely used and popular.[14] These concepts are still popular and widely used.

The English word *strategy* comes from the ancient Greek *strategos*—the strategist. The above mentioned war council met in a building in Athens that was built next to the city walls, not downtown by the Acropolis, to strategize. Its flat roof was the same height as the walls from which the generals looked out on the fields surrounding the city to see what challenge was approaching them. They could also turn around and look within the city to see what resources they had internally to deal with the enemy outside the walls. The term "strategy" is simply "the generals' view." The view—what they saw—was then used to plan what to do, the next move, in order to ensure power or the acquired competitive advantage. A simple shorthand is that strategy is fundamentally *who, what, when, where, why, how,* and *how much.*

Within the academic world of strategy, there has been considerable debate about whether strategy really is planning, what this planning activity really is all about, and whether firms really should plan so much about the future in the first place.[15] We argue that part of strategy, strategizing, and strategic management certainly involves planning, and especially for starting firms, planning is important. This may be more of a process of emergent strategy as the entrepreneur is so resource constrained and the firm so fragile that to anticipate every contingency would be impossible, but not anticipating obvious obstacles is foolish. We hold the view that strategy making is a major fact-finding exercise that is necessary to avoid maximizing unpleasant surprises that come from acting in total ignorance. Most starting firms and entrepreneurs have far too little information about their business and markets, and many of the "if we had only known" situations may have never taken place. Therefore, planning is a systematic way of thinking about and acting on the future. It is a way of enacting the future and in some ways an attempt to design parts of the future. While most of us do not know anything about the true future, planning can heighten certain preparedness. It becomes a way of preempting the undesirable and a way of attempting to control what can be controlled. Despite all this, it is necessary to keep in mind that many things are beyond control and surprise, and there is a great deal of fortuity in the courses lives and businesses take. That is why we say that entrepreneurial strategies are often emergent.

THE FUNCTION OF STRATEGY IN ENTREPRENEURIAL COMPANIES

Strategy has been defined in many ways in literature. For our purpose, to build an entrepreneurial strategy that will enable an entrepreneur to launch a venture and sustain the activity, we use a definition, originally given by Finnish professor Juha Näsi and here freely translated from Finnish to English.[16] To our minds, this definition describes and captures the purpose of a strategy: Strategy is the plot of the action, the common thread of a firm's action.

Strategy holds the future story of the firm; if the thread is broken into pieces, so will the story and the firm's future be, too. Strategy is the master screenplay, and we all know what a film with a poor screenplay is—not a box-office success even if it is full of special effects! Accordingly, strategy provides management and employees with a general, broad sense of direction of the venture. It helps bind the team together. It should create both a sense of purpose for what is going on in terms of specific activities and should foster commitment on the part of all involved in the firm. A company needs a mission and a vision statement, but in addition to that it also needs a strategic plan that will translate these into specific action steps. For a strategic plan to be of any help in the venture-creating process, it has to be communicated to those involved in the firm. It is reasonable to consider a strategy totally proprietary to the firm, but if the owner keeps it a private secret, it is highly unlikely it will ever be implemented. That is, it is not enough to give the lines in the play to the actors—the whole story has also to be told to the actors, otherwise everybody and everything will be hopelessly disconnected and not function in concert. In other words, do not keep the strategy to yourself!

A strategy supports the process of developing value from identified opportunities and evolves continuously through new opportunities. A strategy is not engraved in granite on the wall, but is a living blueprint that changes to reflect the changing external world. Strategy is value based, focusing on creating value through innovation and opportunity. Strategy must be emergent, as you cannot always predict when or where innovations will occur. Thus, a strategy cannot be very specific, but the detailed action plans to achieve specific goals can be specific. Strategy evolves, in part, from the firm's own actions as they will change and impact the external world.

An effective strategy differentiates a firm, exploits its core competencies, and helps build new competencies. It is necessary to understand the strengths and weaknesses of a firm. It is important to recognize the areas that need to be developed in order to stay in business and that there is a continuous need for investing in innovation. This implies continuous search for opportunities and to always be value oriented.

The fundamental task for a firm is to "create" a customer, and that is done through marketing and innovation. A strategy should tell how the firm does, develops, and retains its customers. A strategy should enable a firm to grow without stumbling on its own success. A box-office success is the dream, but too rapid a growth can effectively end the venture before it even takes off. Nothing will kill you *deader* than success.

One key function of the strategy process is to enable the entrepreneur and others in the firm to fully understand the business, the industry, and competition. For the Greeks to understand what was going on, the war council climbed up on the roof to look outside. We think it is very important to note that the view should first be external, to what is going on in the external world, be it the enemy in the field, the industry, the competition, or the marketplace to be served. Only when the external world is understood can an accurate assessment of the interior be made, to assess one's own competitive position as a venture and what will need to be added or changed in order to survive in the marketplace.

Most textbooks use the term "SWOT analysis" (Strengths, Weaknesses, Opportunities, and Threats). This would mean that the starting point is one's strengths and weaknesses (internal qualities), as if they are more important. The problem is that what can be defined as a strength or a weakness depends almost entirely on what happens in the external world. Therefore, we argue that an external analysis determining the threats and opportunities should be assessed first.

The SWOT analysis is a simple, very effective, and probably one of the older tools in strategic management, whose basic idea can be traced back to Selznick's book, *Leadership in Administration*.[17] However, we would, following the Greeks, firmly argue for a TOWS analysis. It is not because we are fond of tossing letters around creating new acronyms, but because we think it is essential for an entrepreneur to work the game plan in this order.

The TOWS analysis will help an entrepreneur understand where and how revenues can be created as well as where the firm can create value for the customer. Four basic questions need to be asked:

1. What are the opportunities?
2. What are the threats?
3. What are the strengths?
4. What are the weaknesses?

Threats and opportunities exist outside the firm; that is, the answers should be found analyzing the industry and the business system (Figure 6.1). Often people list internal weaknesses as threats or internal strengths as potential opportunities, but those provide the wrong answers to the first two questions. The strengths and weaknesses in turn are internal qualities or disabilities of a firm, that is, the inner circle in Figure 6.1. A firm's strengths and weaknesses will convey in what way the firm is capable to act on the market—if it can differentiate, excel, compete, and ultimately exist.

KEY ISSUES IN THE INDUSTRY ENVIRONMENT

In Chapter 2 we used Figure 2.2 to describe networking; here the same figure provides a guide for analyzing the firm's external environment.

When looking at the industrial or sector environment, it is necessary to consider what is known as Porter's Five Forces:[18]

1. New firms entering
2. The power of suppliers
3. The substitutes for products and services
4. The power of buyers
5. The relationships of existing firms

NEW FIRMS

While a starting firm in itself is a new firm in the business environment, the newcomer has to realize that there are other new firms entering. If the entire

FIGURE 6.1
The Firm in the Business System (See Figure 2.2)

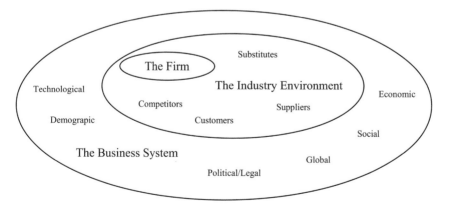

industry is in a massive expansion, this may not be very visible, but in a stable industry—almost stagnated—a new entrant is always very visible. In the dot-com era, new firms entered with a stunning speed and force. At first the markets appeared infinite, but as we know, there is a carrying capacity for every market,[19] and the "excess weight" gained will have to be trimmed in a harsh way. Just how many electronic marketplaces can the Internet economy support? Therefore, it is important to consider how one's firm will be affected by new technology, other new firms, and changes in market demand. How well can the new firm minimize the impact of traditional economies of scale? Moreover, a new firm often faces the legitimacy challenge. That is, will customers believe the claims of product or service differentiation? Is the firm capable of meeting the capital requirements that existing firms currently need to survive and grow? If the firm has cost advantages, how lasting is that advantage, is it sustainable? Will conditions change in a way that improves competitors' access to marketing channels? Finally, is government policy toward competition in the industry likely to change and will this change benefit existing firms or new ones?

SUPPLIERS

Every new venture needs to work with suppliers, who can exert a great deal of influence on a new firm. A new venture has to be very much aware of the stability, size, and composition of supplier groups. What is the strategy of the suppliers doing as a part of their own strategy? Are there any suppliers likely to attempt forward (or backward) integration into the industry, and how will that impact the industry and a new venture? How dependent will a firm be on one or two suppliers in the future? Are other suppliers available?

SUBSTITUTES

It is also important to remember that there are substitute products and services for whatever is offered on the market. For example, the television is a substitute for going to the movies. The Internet is partially also a substitute for the television. Therefore, it is important to consider how likely new substitutes are to occur and in what way will they compete on price or adding other compelling value. A firm needs to consider what actions it can take to reduce the potential of having alternative products seen as legitimate substitutes. This is especially the case when technologies start to merge, as they are in telecommunications and entertainment.

CUSTOMERS

Entrepreneurs sometimes forget, or simply do not realize, that customers can be very powerful. They can go somewhere else or refuse to buy what is sold. It is necessary to anticipate how customers will react to attempts by a firm to differentiate its products or services.

RIVALRY (AND WAR)

In every industry there is rivalry. Just look at the level of competition between airlines for passengers or the competition for buyers interested in a hamburger at lunch. As a new firm it is important to look for shifts in the strategies of major competitors. They sometimes try to undo the established balance of power in an industry. Moreover, industry-wide growth patterns can impact a firm; for example, if the growth in an industry is slowing, it is possible that competition will get fiercer. New firms (mice) can get squeezed when dinosaurs (big, old firms) measure their internal strength. Small firms may be stepped on simply by accident. Especially in a situation where there is excess capacity, there are also firms that are capable of withstanding intensified price competition. Therefore it is part of an entrepreneur's and manager's homework to learn to find out what the unique objectives and strategies of their major competitors are.

THE BUSINESS SYSTEM: EXTERNAL WORLD AND THE FIRM

Trends are important when developing the business concept, the choice of new products and services as well as the strategy of the firm. For an entrepreneur it is essential to develop a routine and a way to constantly scan the external world. This external world is not just the state where the firm is located or the neighboring states or even the United States—it is trends in a much larger context, *global*. Currently, you may want to follow what takes place in Asia or other emerging markets. It is important to find mechanisms for reading a broad array of newspapers, and professional and trade publications to stay abreast of the trends in the external world that impact your industry and business. Today, the Internet provides an efficient helping hand in this respect as most papers provide online issues, but what is more, the Internet provides easy access to many statistical databases, free of charge, and by possessing elementary skills in conducting effective Internet searches. The aim is to get used to monitoring various forces in the environment that impact business success.

Many seem to think that economic trends are the only ones that need monitoring. However, there are basically seven trend categories that have to be analyzed. These are (1) economic, (2) demographic, (3) technological, (4) political, (5) social, (6) global, and (7) local.

Interestingly, demographic changes are rarely dramatic and in most countries there is very detailed information on characteristics of its population.

However, firms rarely utilize this source of information. Other trends that are of basic interest in a served market are changes in Gross Domestic Product, annual economic growth, interest rates, national and local unemployment rates, income levels, immigration patterns, population shifts, lifestyle changes, health trends, environmental concerns, changes in legislation, housing patterns, welfare, and education. Moreover, it is important to consider the source of information, its potential bias. For example, many of the studies published by OECD, concerning the economic state of a particular nation, are based on information provided by that same particular nation. Hence the objectivity of that information can and should be treated with caution.

Our recommendation is that any entrepreneur should identify two or three in each category that can have a major impact on a business and any future products and services. These should then be monitored regularly and in some detail. Finally, it is necessary to remember that almost every trend has a countertrend. A good example is the trend of diets like Atkins or South Beach, and the countertrend is represented by the fact that steakhouse restaurants are still one of the fastest growing segments of the casual dining industry in the United States.

TRENDS IN THE GLOBAL ECONOMY

Two long-standing trends have affected technology entrepreneurship and innovation: (1) technological leadership shifts and (2) concentration of world capital formation.

The patterns of technological leadership have changed many times in the past century. Before World War II, technology leadership was equally shared by Asia, Europe, and the United States. Europe had a lead in a wide range of products and technologies, but not after the exodus of some of the best scientists from Europe to the United States (e.g., Einstein) around 1940. During and after World War II, technology leadership came to be dominated by the United States. What many people do not realize is that from approximately 1965 a swing in the opposite direction began and today technology leadership is more and more equally shared by Asia, Europe, and the United States. If we only consider technology patents as a percentage of the size of the population, countries like Finland and Australia are becoming major players. Just think what the engineers from India and China will develop as these countries are producing the vast majority of new engineers globally.

While technology may be more widely spread, we still have the trend of world capital being concentrated in the United States. For example, the US capital market accounts for 40 percent, the French capital market accounts for 4 percent, and the Italian capital market accounts for 1 percent. There is, of course, an interesting countertrend: European capital markets are consolidating, and with the euro you are beginning to see increased investments across borders in Europe, especially within northern Europe and the Nordic countries. There are some who say that there is a shift in the focus of multinational investment and that the size of the European capital market will grow to at least 40 percent of the world's capital. This is important because large markets tend to favor venture initiation and thus generate start-ups. Large capital markets favor major companies which accelerate both acquisition and spin-off rates.

GENERAL BUSINESS TRENDS

During the dot-com era, considering what was driving business changed to be market share rather than profitability. Today, profitability is again the focus of business (and right so, too). Hence it is highly likely that trends shift what is valued as important. Nevertheless, there are four basic long-term trends for all businesses. First, success requires a customer focus. Second, competition is global. For the entrepreneur this becomes a marketing challenge as the structures of markets are not yet global, for example, a pregnancy test. The UK market is highly concentrated in one or two players, but in the French market it is controlled by a French firm, while in the Spanish market it is controlled by government, and in the US market it is a grocery product. Third, quality is the most important competitive tool and new ventures will lose if they do not grasp it as being critical. Finally, technology is restructuring business not just in terms of products but also in terms of distribution, business processes, marketing, and so on.

LEGAL STRUCTURES

Let us now turn to a discussion of legal structures and intellectual property with their associated regulations, as these are part of the external world. People wishing to start a firm often do not give the legal environment sufficient thought when putting their firms together. Industries and investors all have their favorite legal forms, and discussions of legal matters are really how the external rules of playing the game impact a business. Every entrepreneur needs to understand the legal landscape of his industry. Legal issues and intellectual property are critical parts of a competitive strategy for an entrepreneur. It is essential for a firm to have access to good legal advice. Finding good lawyers is a task for an entrepreneur's networking efforts. Moreover, in the United States the importance of legal advice cannot be underestimated, whereas it may not be that central in, for example, the Nordic countries.

Nevertheless, you are still going to need to understand legal structures and issues as your potential investors are going to expect you to know this part of the external world. For a more detailed understanding of the legal aspects of a new venture and its governance (in the United States), the reader can see Truitt's[20] volume in this series or other books that discuss the details of the legal environment of business.[21] While each country has its own specific legal forms of organization, in North America, Europe, and Australia–New Zealand there are similar forms that have many of the same characteristics. Here are the legal forms we find in the United States, and each has its value and weaknesses:

- Sole Proprietorship
- Partnership
- General Partnership
- Limited Partnership
- Sub-Chapter S corporation
- C corporation
- Limited Liability Company (LLC)

It is important to realize every country and even locales have their own requirements for setting up a business. Remember, they also want to collect tax revenues and protect the consumer of your goods and services.

LEGAL FORMATIONS

There are four clusters of legal forms a business can take.

PROPRIETORSHIP

Proprietorship is one owner with complete control over the venture. The advantage to this form is easy establishment. Please note this still requires local licenses and possible filing of a fictitious name statement. The major disadvantage is that you are personally liable for all risks associated with the business (debts, contracts, etc.). We frankly never recommend this form unless you are perhaps a business consultant with no employees, and even then it may not be a good idea. What is interesting is that this is the dominant form for most small businesses.

PARTNERSHIPS

Partnerships consist of people who combine assets to form a business. They are typically bound by a partnership contract (samples are available in most legal-form books) that dictates, among other things, how profits and liabilities are to be assigned between the partners. A limited liability partnership is similar to the general partnership described above, but it allows for limited partners who do not actively participate in the management of the business and whose personal assets are protected to the level of the investment. You will see this form in everything from Texas oil well deals, to movies, to venture capital funds where there are general and limited partners. You will even see large firms go into partnerships with other large firms and sometimes with smaller firms.

CORPORATIONS

Corporations are the most common form of business. A corporation is considered an entity independent from its owners. That is, it is legally a "person." There are two possible forms of corporation: a C corporation and an S corporation, the latter of which is fundamentally a tax event. The profits of a C corporation are taxed once at the corporate rate and then again at the individual rate when they are dispersed to the owners. An S corporation, however, is not double taxed. Its profits flow directly to the owners (as with proprietorships and partnerships) and are only taxed once, at the individual rate. Most businesses are C corporations. A business must meet certain requirements in order to qualify for S corporation status: the company must be domestic, it must have only voting, owners must be individuals, and no nonresident aliens may own stock. Frankly, this was the primary legal vehicle of entrepreneurial firms until the development of the LLC.

LIMITED LIABILITY COMPANY

A Limited Liability Company (LLC) is fundamentally a combination of the good parts of a partnership and those of a C or S corporation. It pays taxes as a partnership, but provides the same ownership protection as a corporation. As with any legal issue, get good advice and make sure that the form you choose is consistent with the strategy of your firm.

LEGAL STRUCTURES AND STRATEGY

It is important to note that legal structure has an enormous impact on the strategy, especially the financial strategy, that you will use to run your venture. For example, legal structure impacts how you share ownership; how you will get money into your firm; who will give you money; how you will control the firm; and how you get yourself or your money out of the firm at harvest time. For most high-growth firms, entrepreneurs will choose either a C corporation or increasingly an LLC designation. For either, you should have a board to help in the governance of the firm. From all the evidence we have, it is generally agreed that the more successful firms have an active board of directors or at an earlier stage a board of advisors. The critical issue is to get outside advice and counsel. Remember this is another lesson of networking. The value of a board is to help in the effective governance of the business, by helping in the separation of ownership and management (especially if you have outside investors). In the longer run it helps in value maximization, and can help in succession that can come from unexpected events like an untimely death. I will discuss boards later again when discussing management issues.

STATUTORY BOARDS

The question we are often asked is what kind of directors an entrepreneurial firm should have. First, understand that there are different kinds of legal requirements for a private firm versus a public traded company. In many cases you are legally required to have a board of directors, and our view is if you are going to go through the steps, use that effort to benefit the firm. Frankly a board can serve as an independent forum for you to discuss issues you might not want to discuss with employees. Boards assure the continuation of the firm in case something happens to you, by serving as the steward of all shareholders' assets. We believe it encourages quality improvements. We are going to go into greater detail on boards later. What is forgotten is that they serve other functions:

- Alert and monitor management
- Provide advice and counsel
- Legitimize company, promote it, and add credibility and image
- Approve objectives and policies
- Reinforce the professional management of closely held firms
- Resolve conflicts and sensitive matters—often involving family
- Act in a crisis (CEO incapacity, merger, or major legal attack)
- Represent the noninvolved shareholders
- Special consulting assignments (expertise)

INTELLECTUAL PROPERTY

While we are not intellectual property lawyers, we think every entrepreneur needs to understand what intellectual property is and how to protect it because it may be a critical part of competitive advantages. When we think about some of the more interesting patents, one is immediately reminded of the one click–shopping model of Amazon.com that helped them be one of the first profitable Internet firms. Google's patents are estimated to be worth millions to both the firm and Stanford University, which licenses some of these to the firm. Simply intellectual property is property resulting from intellectual activities. These can include inventions (mechanical, electrical, chemical); computer software; manufacturing processes; designs, business models (in the United States); and genetic materials. One goes about the protection of intellectual property through trade secrets, patents, copyrights, and trademarks.

PATENTS

A patent is a constitutionally guaranteed right to exclude others from making, selling, or using the patented invention in the United States (or country of issue). It is granted for twenty years (fourteen years for design patents). A patent does not give the right to use or practice the invention. It may be used to "keep exclusive," license, "sit-on," and not use. I remember when one razor-blade company wanted to buy the license to the patent for laser hair removal, all they wanted to do was sit on the patent. Remember where they make their money: razor blades. Exclusive right even applies to independent, parallel inventions. To be frank you will discover that if you ever go on www.uspo.org you will sometimes find dozens of patents to achieve the same end. Simply a patent defines the limits of the intellectual property rights for an invention. Essentially it is a deed to that particular invention, not necessarily the end result. Patents are bound by the claims defined by the patent. Language in the application (specification and claims) is very important. Get professional help, do not try to do this yourself, but be actively involved in the process.

PATENTABLE

Fundamentally what is patentable is determined by three tests. First is *novelty*: the invention must be new and novel. The second is *nonobviousness*: the invention must be nonobvious in light of existing art. Third is *enablement*, which means that the description in patent must enable one "skilled in the art" to practice the invention. There can be no secret steps. The key is to remember that an idea or concept is not patentable until it is reduced to practice. Do not expect to do this process by yourself. We strongly recommend you find a patent attorney who knows your area of technology and with whom you feel comfortable. Expect that, your patent application will be rejected on your first reading as upward of 95 percent of applications are rejected at the first submission. Carefully read the examiners' comments and address these in the next submission. We personally believe you should be aggressive in your patent claims to get as broad a claim as possible. This process, however, is not cheap in time or money. Expect it to take at least a year and to cost at least $20,000 if not more in the United States. We strongly recommend exploring key international patents in the European Union and in Asia, especially Japan (depending on the technology). This will cost even more. The decision to patent or not is really the discussion of a cost-benefit analysis and how the patents best fit within your overall firm strategy.

PATENT STRATEGY

It is important that you have a patent strategy that is tied to the strategy of your firm if you are in the business of creating new technology. Please remember that for US patent filing it must occur within one year of any printed disclosure. However, in Europe if you have disclosed you have lost your right to a patent. The resulting rule is simple: file for a patent before you disclose, use in anyway other than testing or offer for sale. Our second rule is likewise be sure to keep accurate records of when you discover, or invent. Follow the guidelines of engineers and scientists and keep a bound log of your work. Important discoveries should be countersigned or even notarized as to date. You need to be able to provide documentation of invention. Such documentation identifies statutory bar dates and identifies potential prior art that has been overcome. Please remember to put in all those who have really contributed to the invention. This is not a place to put your spouse as an inventor simply to make them feel good. Remember that patents can be a source of income from licensing and cross-licensing. Some technology firms actually make money simply by being R&D houses. This is typical especially in biotechnology. In summary, timing is critical and missing deadlines can result in the loss of patentability. If it seems new, does something better, or both, it is probably patentable.

TRADEMARKS

Trademarks and logos for a firm are important in branding your business, and you need to realize that laws govern these as well. We remember a young woman who wanted to open a café to learn that the name she chose (although her name) was the same as that of a major international electronics firm. After an expensive court battle, she discovered she could not use the name. Why was this the case? Because a trademark is anything that implies an origin, source, nature, or quality of goods (products) or services.

Trademarks have a base in common law. There are "Springing Rights" based on use. Trademarks are owned by the user and can be assigned with goodwill. Trademarks have no limit to them unlike patents, which have a twenty-year limit. Trademarks like SONY or MICKEY MOUSE are protected by firms, especially when someone might use a trademark name that creates confusion. If you use the mouse and do not have the permission of the Disney Company, you will learn the hard way how people protect trademarks. If there is confusion, then you are in the world of trademark infringement litigation. If you can demonstrate damage then you can take infringer's profits, payment for damages sustained, and treble damages for willful infringement. The rule here is be careful and do your homework on logos, names, and so on.

COPYRIGHTS

A copyright is an exclusive right to reproduce a work in a tangible medium of expression. This can be a work of art, music, software, a book, and so on. A copyright is also the right to make derivative works. It has quasi-springing rights. Violation of a copyright occurs not only when there is a direct infringement (you copy the work exactly) but also when there is substantial similarity. The critical issue about copyrights is that the author owns the property absent assignment of work for hire. "Work for Hire" is statutory and is not common sense. If you subcontract for someone to write say computer code, they need to assign that work to you unless you are a formal employer of the author. This is one of the trade-offs of using subcontractors. Make sure you get assignment of the intellectual property you contracted for and that such is designated in the employment contracts of those you hire. We have seen a large number of software firms that hired outside contractors to write codes and that do not get the assignment of ownership. Just because you hire an Indian software engineer in Mumbai to write the code does not mean you own it.

TRADE SECRETS

When one thinks of trade secrets we usually think of the formula for Coca-Cola. Trade secrets are anything not generally available in public domain that provides a competitive value. Trade secrets must be protected like any other proprietary object. Unlike patents and copyrights, trade secrets are primarily based on common law and state statute. It is important that you take active care of trade secrets in your firm, especially things like client lists. Do not claim a trade secret if anyone can get it off the back of the Nestle chocolate chip bag.

Checklist for Competition and Industry

Now that we have reviewed the external world, and especially the legal side, we can write that section of your business plan. Remember that writing a business plan is a contact sport as is everything else in being an entrepreneur. Think of the checklist on competition as a set of questions or statements and have you answered these in the process of writing this section of the plan.

1. List direct competition by product and geographic market: Who is directly seeking the same money you are (e.g., specialty retail stores compete with specialty stores, not department stores)?

2. List the indirect competitors by product and geographic market (e.g., movie theaters are indirect competitors of video stores).

3. List emerging competitors entering the industry or market (e.g., video rental stores, supermarkets entering video business).

4. Describe the competitors' strengths and weaknesses by product and market segment: List in chart form, tie these back to your strengths and weaknesses.

5. Describe the competitors' share of the market by product: List by percentages or in unit or dollar volume.

6. Discuss relevant background information concerning major competitors: Include profiles of their management team, company history, and financials; show where they are strong or weak.

7. On what basis will the product/service compete with them? Consider product superiority, price, advertising, and so on.

8. How is this venture superior to that of the competition? Consider operations, management, product/service, price, service, delivery, and so on.

9. How does this product/service compare to competition in the eyes of customers? Include some customer reactions from a small sample you have taken.

10. Do you threaten the major strategic objectives or self-image of competition? Will they attempt to destroy the venture at any cost?

11. If the competition tries to destroy your position in the marketplace, how will you retaliate? What marketing exclusionary tactics can you anticipate?

12. List sources to evaluate product/services against competition: Agencies, individual firms, publications, and so on; include statements and testimonials.

13. What is the basis upon which the industry competes? Consider price, quality, promotion, personal selling, innovation, legal, franchises, and so on.

14. What has been the history of the industry treatment of new enterprises? How easy is it to enter the industry?

15. What has been the fate of new firms in the industry? Have other new firms successfully entered the industry?

16. What are the entry barriers? What keeps others out?
17. What are the exit barriers? What will keep you and others from leaving?

HELPFUL HINTS

Here we are going to sound a bit like a preacher. To most entrepreneurs, what they experience in starting and growing a company is almost totally new. Remember while it is new to you it is not new to the world. Use your network and find a mentor, someone who has been where you are going. Planning is key and a written plan is better. Be willing to supplement your team's skills and your skills with a board of directors. Consider making your mentor a member of your board, but make sure they know how to develop strategic business plans. Do not try to do everything yourself. Be willing to form joint ventures, strategic partnerships, and the like. Cooperate with other firms in mutually beneficial relationships even while competing with them in other areas. The bottom line is to go where you want to and set your sights a bit high. Remember that each organization has its core competencies and incompetencies. To us the biggest incompetency is death by nonopportunity, that is by *not* making choices. Another is analysis paralysis (a long-standing disease of the American MBA) or which we call the fear of opportunity. Likewise, avoid not changing focus as the world changes. Finally, opportunity costs are relevant in good times. You do not want to slow sales down in a sellers' market as high margins will cover inefficiencies. Cash costs are relevant in bad times. Remember, as an entrepreneur you need to be like Benjamin Franklin, the first great American entrepreneur, who said, *a penny saved is a penny earned.* Watch your pennies while making investments in products in a buyers' market.

NOTES

1. Stephen Cummings, "Brief Case: The First Strategist," *Long Range Planning* 26 (1993): 133–135; Juha Näsi and Manu Aunola, *Yritysten strategiaprosessit, yleinen teoria ja suomalainen käytäntö* (The Strategy Process of Corporations: General Theory and Finnish Practice) (Helsinki: MET, 2001); Nicolò Machiavelli, *The Prince and the Discourses* (New York: Modern Library, 1950); Sun Tzu, *The Art of War* (New York: Oxford University Press, 1971).

2. Kenneth R. Andrews, *The Concept of Corporate Strategy* (Homewood, IL: Dow Jones-Irwin, 1971), 26.

3. Rick Levine, Christoffer Locke, Doc Searls, and David Weinberger, *The Cluetrain Manifesto* (Cambridge, MA: Perseus Publishing, 2000), 78.

4. Cummings, "Brief Case: The First Strategist."

5. Petronius Arbiter, who served under Nero, stated in *Satyricon* (83:192).

6. Näsi and Aunola, *Yritysten strategiaprosessit*, 9.

7. Ellen E. Chaffee, "Tree Models of Strategy," *Academy of Management Review* January 10, 1985, 89–98; Daniel R. Gilbert, Edwin Hartman, John J. Mauriel, and R. Edward Freeman, *A Logic for Strategy* (Cambridge, MA: Ballinger, 1988); Gerry Johnson and Kevan Scholes, *Exploring Corporate Strategy* (London: Prentice Hall, 1993); Bengt Karlöf, *Business Strategy in Practice* (Hoboken, NJ: John Wiley & Sons, 1987); Henry Mintzberg, "Strategy Formation Schools of Thought," in *Perspectives on Strategic Management*, ed. J. W. Fredrickson (New York: Harper Business, 1991), 105–236; Henry Mintzberg, Bruce Ahlstrand, and Joseph Lampel, *Strategy Safari* (New York: Free Press, 1998); Juha Näsi, *Arenas of Strategic Thinking* (Helsinki: Helsinki Foundation of Economic Education, 1991); Juha Näsi, Petri Laine, and Juha Laine, "Strategy Logic in a Mega Leader Company," University of Jyväskylä Department of Economics and Management, Reprint Series, No. 43, 1996.

8. Kenneth R. Andrews, *The Concept of Corporate Strategy* (Homewood, IL: Dow Jones-Irwin, 1971); Michael E. Porter, *Competitive Strategy* (New York: Free Press, 1980).

9. Gilbert et al., *A Logic for Strategy*, 5.

10. Arnoldo C. Hax, "Redefining the Concept of Strategy and the Strategy Formation Process," *Planning Review* May/June (1990): 34–40; Henry Mintzberg, "The Strategy Concept 1: Five Ps for Strategy," *California Management Review* 30 (1987): 11–24; Näsi, *Arenas of Strategic Thinking*.

11. Näsi, *Arenas of Strategic Thinking*.

12. Michael E. Porter, "Strategy and the Internet," *Harvard Business Review*, March 2001, 63–77; Porter, "What Is Strategy?" *Harvard Business Review*, November–December 1996, 61–78.

13. Bruce D. Henderson, "The Origin of Strategy," *Harvard Business Review*, November–December 1989, 139–143; Peter F. Drucker, "The New Society of Organizations," *Harvard Business Review*, September–October 1995, 95–104.

14. See, for example, Kenneth R. Andrews, *The Concept of Corporate Strategy* (Homewood, IL: Dow Jones-Irwin, 1971); Igor Ansoff, *Corporate Strategy* (New York: McGraw-Hill Book Company, 1965); Richard N. Anthony, *Planning and Control Systems: A Framework for Analysis* (Cambridge, MA: Harvard University Press, 1965); George A. Steiner, *Top Management Planning* (New York: MacMillan Company, 1969).

15. Henry Mintzberg, *The Rise and Fall of Strategic Planning* (New York: Free Press, 1994).

16. See, for example, Näsi and Aunola, *Yritysten strategiaprosessit*.

17. Philip Selznick, *Leadership in Administration: A Sociological Interpretation* (Evanston, IL: Row Peterson, 1957); Mintzberg, *Rise and Fall of Strategic Planning*.

18. Porter, *Competitive Strategy*.

19. Howard E. Aldrich, *Organizations Evolving* (London: Sage Publications, 1999).

20. Wesley B. Truitt, *The Corporation* (Westport, CT: Greenwood Press, 2006).

21. Frank B. Cross and Roger L. Miller, *West's Legal Environment of Business*, 5th ed. (Mason, OH: Thomson South-Western, 2004).

Seven

The Market and Customer Groups

In this chapter we continue to look at the external world, this time your customers.[1] This is perhaps one of the most critical areas for any entrepreneur to understand.[2] When you look at your customers it is necessary to look beyond your own experiences as a potential customer. We have previously encouraged the use of external data sources to learn about the market—but at some point it becomes necessary to get a closer view. A demanding way is to actually collect fresh primary data. That may not be completely avoidable, but before that, taking a serious and honest look at oneself in the mirror is a cheap and very informative procedure. This is a mixture of relying on one's own instinct and at the same time closely analyzing what one does, why, and when. That means one assumes the "character of the average"—and in most cases it will be quite true. It is a way of expanding the understanding about what the market is like and what the customers' needs, wants, and fears are.[3]

The Internet and Google are instrumental for a quick first look, but it is not enough to truly understand your market.[4] It is important for any entrepreneur to conduct both primary and secondary market research on the concept. The first way would be to stop and talk to a real customer—it may sound strange, but many entrepreneurs rarely asked ordinary persons of their opinion. Do not assume you know what customers really want or how it is easy to obtain customers.

A key part of marketing is public relations and advertising. Effective marketing is dependent on how active the entrepreneur is in the process. Nevertheless, marketing can be very expensive and ineffective, or surprisingly cost effective. To achieve the latter an entrepreneur needs to focus and match budget resources (money, time, and personnel) to a defined marketing plan. Perhaps, one of the most important issues and the most difficult one is to understand who the target audience of all marketing efforts is. What are their needs, wants, and fears?

KNOWING THE CUSTOMER

One of the most important things for an entrepreneur is to know the customer, whether it is a business, an industry, a government, or an individual. In fact there is no way of knowing too much about a customer—but most entrepreneurs often know far too little. A simple way is to generate a list of what customers need, want, and fear with respect to the offered product or service. This is a process of stepping into the shoes of the other person. Within information systems a similar method is known as a cognitive *walk-through*, that is, a person walks through a situation explaining every step. This is, indeed, very time consuming but extremely informative. The aim of this is to identify the areas in which current products or services fall short. What do customers seek? As one colleague expressed it, when asked who to hire, which was drawing on the fears of the customer, "I will give you a list of who NOT to hire because of bad service."

It is important to explore how customers perceive a company, product, or service with respect to competition. It is vital to learn to listen to the "voice" of the customer. The voice will reveal opinions, reasons, and desired solutions (customers' needs, wants, and fears). Not surprisingly, women are generally better at this than men. Moreover, most customers live in a different world than the entrepreneur and speak a different language; that is, they do not necessarily speak the industry's jargon.

It is necessary to group needs, wants, and fears into strategic bundles to get a sense of the relative importance of them in order to focus the firm's efforts on what is important. To do this properly, market research is instrumental. The reason why it is important to categorize the market and conduct at least some market research is shown in Table 7.1.[5] This provides some key information about distributors, that is, who would potentially distribute a product. This is not a count of how many; it is to show what a complex reality an entrepreneur will face. For foreign entrepreneurs considering entering the US market, the information in Table 7.1 comes as a fundamental surprise. The surprise lies in the size of the numbers.

MARKET RESEARCH

The best thing—if affordable—would be to conduct a rigorous market research, but most starting entrepreneurs cannot afford it, yet it would be an elementary insurance. Therefore, it is important to learn to obtain quick customer input. Again, the Internet is an affordable friend, but only if you can distinguish good information from bad! Somebody in the firm will have to know how to create, interpret, and analyze a market research survey. The best would be if there were some statistical skills in the firm in order to understand conjoint and cluster analysis, but since this is highly unlikely, the best advice

TABLE 7.1

Some Examples of Direct Selling Points in the United States, by Category

Category	
Eating places	286,000
Grocery stores	132,000
Auto repair garages	112,000
Women's dress shops	51,000
Drug stores (chemists, pharmacies)	50,000
Auto parts and supply stores	43,000
Hotels and motels	39,000
Shoe stores	37,000
Furniture stores	30,100
Liquor stores	30,000
Lumber and building supply stores	27,000
Sporting goods stores	21,000
Hardware stores	19,000
Consumer electronic stores	16,000

Source: Tim P. Beane, and Daniel M. Ennis, "Marketing Segmentation: A Review," *European Journal of Marketing*, 1987, 21(5), 20-42.

is to use resources of either professional market survey firms or, for example, the marketing students of a nearby university.[6]

MARKETING TERMINOLOGY

It is important to offer some definition of five very important marketing concepts that often get mixed up or reduced to one single concept called *market*. It is essential for any entrepreneur to distinguish between these concepts when assessing the market and its real potential. Often one hears people saying, "China is our market," or "We will enter the US market." This may be true for giant corporations like GE or Nokia, but hardly so for a starting entrepreneur. This is also sometimes called the Chinese Glove problem: "If we can only sell one glove to every Chinese or if we can only catch 1 percent of the US market we will make all the money we need, look at the money I would make!" The truth is more likely that a customer is a particular area or even a particular segment of the market. The problem is that hardly every Chinese can afford a glove, want a glove, or have the possibility to buy one. Also, a goal to catch only 1 percent of a market will not impress partners or financers as the reality will most likely be only a fraction of the goal.[7] Therefore, it is very important to understand the meaning of these five terms.

1. *Market* means the set of all actual and potential buyers of a product. This is what is often also called "the theoretical market size," which means that the firm

catches every single person. For example, there are 5.2 million people living in Finland. The theoretical market—the market—for televisions would be 5.2 million. In reality it is approximately 2 million as most families have one set and a family consists of on average four persons. Even if some families have several sets, there are many, perhaps surprisingly, who do not have a TV set. Another example would be assessing the incidences and prevalence of a disease worldwide, thus assuming that once a cure is found *every* person with the disease will get a cure.

2. *Potential market* is what most people mean when they use the word "market." The potential market is the set of customers who profess a sufficient level of interest in the product or service offered. For example, Finland will transfer to digital TV broadcasting as of August 1, 2007. Vendors of digital TV sets and the so-called digital boxes that enable old TVs to broadcast digitally have therefore concluded that the potential market is approximately 2 million since the analogue broadcasting will end and vendors assume that everyone with a TV today will want to continue watching on August 1, 2007. The problem here is for the vendor to assess how many will buy a new digital TV and how many will just buy the "box." With respect to the disease example, the problem is captured in the relative prevalence; that is, a disease is more common in certain areas and countries. Some diseases do not actually exist in certain countries. Moreover, the market potential is impacted by a number of other factors, such as the health-care system of the country. Some may not have the income to take advantage of the new cure.

3. *Available market* is that set of customers who have interest, income, and access to a particular product or service being offered. With respect to the digital TV problem, it is assumed that the available market equals the potential market; vendors assume that everyone has an interest and income. Availability is guaranteed since the network covers the entire country. With respect to the disease problem, availability is much more complex. For example, when a person is born in Finland or Australia, he or she is immediately part of the social security system, which, among other things, reimburses medical care, both treatment and medication. In the United States approximately 30 percent are not part of a health-care system. Consider yet a third example: a tourist may have visited a restaurant in, let us say, Hania on Crete in Greece. The service was really good, the food was excellent, but it is unlikely that this person would become a frequent customer since the trip lasts a week and next year the vacation is spent in Italy. Availability is unavailable!

4. *Target market* is the market the firm decides to enter or capture. To find out just how large this is, firms often segment the market. Trying to serve or please everyone is a near recipe for failure. The target market is quite often much smaller than market, potential market, and available market. Determining the size of the target market is also impacted by the demand; that is, are there needs, wants, and fears that will translate into a demand for a product or service?

5. *Market demand* is the total volume of a product or service that would be purchased by a *defined* customer group in a *defined* geographical area in a *defined* time period in a *defined* marketing environment under a *defined* marketing program.

To summarize the above, we provide an example out of our experience.

Some years ago we were approached by a research group active in the area of biomaterials. They had developed a material that could be used in dressings (bandages) for treating severe burns. One of the problems, the medical researchers told us, was that dressings stick, and when the patient goes in for operation the dressings have to be removed. This is very painful and traumatic. The new product was nonstick. We were told that the time between the application of the dressings and the actual surgery could be days, sometimes weeks, and during this time the dressings had to be changed many times. The researchers, whose careers dealt totally with medical research rather than treatment, wanted to know the market size, since they were about to start a firm and needed to convince financers. We told them we needed to know more about the problem, that is, how the treatment of burns actually occurred, in order to be able to help.

To do this we contacted a major university hospital. We were met by considerable surprise from treating physicians. We soon understood why. We were told that treatment of severe burns had changed completely. The procedure we had been told by the researchers dated back to some fifteen years. Now a severely burned person undergoes surgery immediately. Hence the problem as described by the researchers no longer exists. In other words, there was no demand for this product for this purpose. That is, the market the researchers had considered to be the one with the greatest potential did not exist. Our questions then became "Is there any demand for nonstick dressings and in what situations would that be?" How large would *that* market, potential market, available market, and target market be? How would possible competition in terms of similar products or substitutes impact demand?

MARKET SEGMENTATION

Market segmentation is a way of categorizing markets based on some specific criteria. To be blunt, everyone needs food, water, and air, but the rest will vary among individuals (including sex). Therefore, to determine target market, market segmentation is needed. Market segmentation aims, in a practical way, at categorizing customers into manageable and addressable groups based on their needs, wants, and fears. It is inefficient and most often not economically possible (or wise) to treat customers as individuals or as one large mass.

Interestingly, herein lies a paradox. Every marketing book will encourage treating customers as individuals, and every one of us knows what a pleasant experience it is when we are served in an individual way and not treated as a large crowd. We all like to think of ourselves as *somebody* and not just *anybody*. But, as this is rarely economically possible, market segmentation is a way to get as close to the individual as possible in an affordable way. The categories should include those customers who respond to a particular offering in similar ways. Primarily, there are four ways to segment a market: geographically, demographically, psychographically, and behaviorally.

GEOGRAPHIC MARKET SEGMENTATION

As mentioned earlier, the Chinese market or the US market is not merely one homogeneous market, nor is Europe or Australia. Many European and Australian companies have made the mistake of treating the United States as one market and therefore failed in their attempt to launch their products in the United States. Similarly, Europe is not just United Kingdom and Germany or France. The Nordic countries may be similar but are also very different. The task is to understand what the similarities and differences mean for the firm. The European Union (EU) is comprised today of twenty-five countries. Which countries do not belong to the EU? Is Norway a member of the EU? Which of the countries that were once Yugoslavia belong to the EU? Not all use the euro as their currency. Does Sweden or Denmark use the euro? What does all this mean for a firm? How many understand that 90 percent of the Australian market essentially exists in eight urban areas? Which are they and where are they?

Similarly, few persons in Europe and Australia realize that the United States can be defined in very different ways. One of the authors (the Finnish one) of this book happens to own a cookbook called *American Food: A Celebration*, which divides the American kitchen into eleven areas (New England, the Middle Atlantic, the South, Louisiana, the Midwest, the Plains States, Texas, the Southwest, the Mountain States, the Pacific Northwest and Alaska, and Hawaii and California). This categorization may seem somewhat unusual, but this is made based on food and taste, which in turn reflects at least some similarity in consumption habits and some cultural similarities that should be of much interest for firms in such industries. But where does the Midwest become the Plains State? Which are the Plains States? Moreover, Louisiana and Texas are treated individually; should this individuality be considered in other areas of consumption as well? What about East Texas that some consider western Louisiana? Is this categorization valid in other industries?

Another example is this one: Pacific, Mountain, West North Central, West South Central, East North Central, East South Central, South Atlantic, Middle Atlantic, and New England. The only similarity between the two is New England. Where does Louisiana or Texas come in this categorization? Those who live in South Florida will most likely claim a difference to those who live in Orlando, Florida. Miami is often called *La Republica* to reflect its Cuban population. The question is whether this difference is significant to a firm.

In geographic segmentation it is also necessary to break down the market by its size; that is, is it urban, suburban, or rural? It may come as a surprise to many, but if we look at the United States or Australia, they are both essentially rural with many vast areas that are scarcely populated, but the urban areas are immensely large and very densely populated. We no longer speak of just metropolis; in fact many metropolitan areas form megalopolis. The fact that these megalopolitan areas exist in the United States leads many to believe that the United States is urban. Hence the geographic area you are targeting is under 5,000, under 20,000, under 50,000, under 5,000,000, and less than 50,000,000. Large urban areas are not always the obvious target markets. For example, Wal-Mart targeted small rural towns and gained dominance there before expanding to larger urban markets. Finally, we can define markets by climate: northern, southern, Mediterranean, or tropical.

DEMOGRAPHIC MARKET SEGMENTATION

Market segmentation by demographic variables is the most common way. These are typically age, gender, occupation, family size, education, nationality, religion, income, and ethnicity. For Europeans the ethnic quilt of the United States sometimes comes as a real surprise. Many are not aware of the large population of Asian descent that exists in the United States, nor are they aware that Hispanics in California and Florida are considered to be of different ethnic backgrounds. For a Scandinavian driving first time in Miami, Florida, the concept of Latin America will stun; the number of Latin American flags in the back window of the cars, flags that prove a potentially immense heterogeneity and prompt an immediate consulting of an encyclopedia of Latin American flags.

Most of the demographic data can be found in a nation's census data, highly detailed information available in most countries. These are what we would call raw data, or raw numbers, because they hide very important information that an entrepreneur needs to know about the customers and the market.

PSYCHOGRAPHIC MARKET SEGMENTATION

The way to get beyond the raw numbers provided by demographic data is to consider psychographic variables. These are normally captured in either lifestyle or personality. Lifestyle segmentation studies hobbies, TV-viewing habits, social activities, club memberships, and vacation preferences. Personality variables are perhaps less clear but provide critical information with respect to certain products and services. These variables are, for example, compulsive, outgoing, authoritarian, ambitious, and the list goes on. The point here is to think about how the customers define themselves or how others in society might define them. Here the use of focus groups can often help you determine what various customer segments are really thinking.

BEHAVIORAL MARKET SEGMENTATION

Behavioral market segmentation targets how customers use the products: regularly or on a special occasion like a wedding. Another way is by user type; for example, are customers nonusers, ex-users, potential users, first-time users, or regular users? Related to user status is usage rate; for example, are user rates light, medium, or heavy? A third way is to look at the loyalty of users; is it absolute, strong, moderate, or none at all?

Additional ways to analyze behavior involve looking at how customers make buying decisions. Are they fast or slow? Do they make independent decisions or are they dependent on opinions from others? Are they unaware, aware, informed, interested, or intend to buy? Are they hostile, negative, indifferent, positive, or enthusiastic to new products? Are they innovators, early adopters, early majority, late majority, or laggard? Do they value quality, service, economy, or speed?

BUSINESS MARKET SEGMENTATION

While the above discussion has focused on consumer markets primarily, the same variables apply to business-to-business markets, although they tend to change somewhat. There are, however, additional ways to segment business markets and these include purchasing approaches, personal characteristics of the decision makers, operating variables of the firms, and even situational factors.[8]

For business markets the demographic variables can be defined as industrial sector, company size, location, and family or nonfamily owned. Examples of operating variables of a client firm could be use of technology, user status, or the capabilities of the client firm. Purchasing approaches include how the purchasing function is organized, the power structure in the firm, the nature of its existing relationships with other suppliers, its general purchasing policies and criteria, and the use of technology.

For example, if you want to do business with Wal-Mart, you had better have all of your inventory and billing systems on line and consistent with those of Wal-Mart or you will not have them for a customer. Segmenting business markets by situational factors includes factors like urgency, the need for a specific application, or the size of order. Finally, firms can be seen to have personalities (of sorts); that is, some firms like to purchase from similar firms (family businesses, for example) or have different attitudes toward risk (some avoid new suppliers), and some operate with a strong sense of loyalty.

While segmentation is important, it is equally important not to oversegment, that is, defining the segments too narrowly. But most segments are dynamic; they change over time and people within one segment may move across to other segments.

SIX MARKETING RULES FOR THE ENTREPRENEURIAL FIRM

Rule 1: *Know the concept and the target.* Learn to know the market, to understand and do direct and primary marketing research.

Rule 2: *Focus.* Remain focused on the market in every respect. This includes advertising and promotional activities.

Rule 3: *Be unique.* Understand your target's needs, wants, and fears. Build a unique position. Know your competition.

Rule 4: *Do not stop.* Repetition is the key to both good marketing strategy and good advertising. Marketing is an investment that takes time. "Word of mouth" or "word of web" are not sufficient means of marketing.

Rule 5: *Know the goals.* Create specific goals for marketing activities with weekly and monthly timelines. Make a road map (your marketing plan, which we will discuss later in the chapter).

Rule 6: *Take action.* Analysis is not enough. Marketing does not happen by itself. It requires that action is taken.

FINAL ADVICE AND STRATEGIC QUESTIONS

Realize that the race is often won by those who are the fastest and the best in getting a new idea to market rather than by those who create the product or service. There is no such thing as first to market advantage. We would like to emphasize *it is first to market acceptance.* If first to market were true, we would all be using Osborne computers as desktops or laptops. Therefore, it is important to create a marketing plan and then implement it. Determine and develop a market niche for your new venture. When establishing marketing alliances (partnerships) with others, make sure that they are win-win. Think of strategic alliance partners as customers. They have needs, wants, and fears, too, concerning their partners.

Expect wins and losses in marketing. In other words, not everything will work. Spend time marketing the concept and the firm to key decision makers; it essentially means spending at least a day a week in marketing the concept.

This includes keeping a high visibility through mailings, community involvement, speeches, articles, and so on. Remember that networking is a form of marketing, so develop meaningful relationships with a wide range of community and business leaders. Remember the "strength of weak ties."

This advice can be summarized in seven questions to be asked about a marketing strategy:

1. What is the purpose of the marketing?
2. How is market penetration going to be achieved by focusing on the firm's strengths?
3. Who is the target audience for the marketing, promotion, and sales activities?
4. What are the marketing tools available?
5. Where are the targets for marketing in the community?
6. What is the management team recognized or admired for doing?
7. Does the budget have sufficient resources in terms of money, time, and personnel?

Checklist for the Marketing Plan

In addition to a business plan, a firm often needs an independent marketing plan. The way to proceed here is to conduct a thorough market analysis based on which a marketing plan is created. In the business plan, an executive summary and the most critical information are then included. It is then possible, upon request, to supplement the entire marketing analysis and plan separately. It is essential that the market analysis and the marketing plan show a real understanding of market needs and that the firm understands its customers. Remember the example above of the nonstick bandages for severe-burn victims.

Below is a checklist, which can be regarded as a set of questions that have to be answered in a way that generates statements about the market. Once again, some of these questions may not apply to your industry, but when relevant they should, of course, be included.

1. List information on the industry that the business will compete in:
   a. current size
   b. growth potential
   c. geographic locations
   d. industry trends
   e. seasonal factors
   f. profit potential

   g. sales patterns (single, bulk, direct, etc.)

   h. development of new products

   i. customers/market

2. What is the profile of the customer or various customer groups?

   a. age

   b. sex

   c. profession

   d. income

   e. psychographic information

   f. geographic location

   g. other demographics

3. Describe the benefits provided for the customer:

   a. Do they differ for customer groups?

   b. How?

   c. Can you do a cost-benefit analysis for the customer?

4. What problems are you solving?

   a. Needs

   b. Wants

   c. Fears

5. Describe the customers' need for the product/service:

   a. How much will they save time or money?

   b. What return will the customers receive on the dollars they spend?

   c. Will they have to change their ways of doing things?

   d. Will they be required to purchase other goods/services to utilize yours?

   e. Will they have to change their work habits?

6. Describe the new venture's market niche:

   a. What is the particular appeal?

   b. Identity or place in the market that the product/service possesses.

7. Describe the target market(s) and the potential dollar volume of each that the business has selected for penetration:

   a. Prioritize the list by naming the best target markets first.

   b. Note that your target market might not be the end user but instead your distribution channels.

8. Describe the approach for selling the product/service to the end user:

   a. distribution channels

   b. sales representatives

     c. direct sales force

     d. direct mail

     e. telemarketing

     f. Internet

9. List the costs for penetrating each target market (and by approach):

     a. dollars, people, and time

     b. sales, lead time needed, and so on

10. What advertising/promotion media will be used for the distribution system and the end users?

     a. Address each area that will be used: radio, newspaper, trade journals and magazines, and/or television advertising.

     b. Include a sample of the advertising (if possible) and list costs.

11. How will the packaging and labeling enhance name identification and brand loyalty?

     a. If possible, include sample of packaging.

12. What kind of service, warranties, and guarantees will be offered?

     a. How will these be promoted?

     b. How many of these will affect profits?

13. What are the reactions to the product/service from prospective customers?

     a. Include any testimonials, market surveys, focus group studies, and so on.

14. State why the market efforts are unique or different from competitors.

15. What is the role of trade shows?

     a. Which trade shows will be best for exhibiting the product/service?

     b. Give name, location, date, booth size, and so on.

16. Explain the opportunities in future markets:

     a. Include size, method of penetration, costs, and so on.

NOTES

1. Phillip Kotler, "A Generic Concept of Marketing," *Journal of Marketing* 36, no. 2 (1972): 46–54.

2. Gerald E. Hills, ed., *Marketing and Entrepreneurship: Research Ideas and Opportunities* (Westport, CT: Quorum Books, 1994).

3. H. Keith Hunt, Jonathan C. Huefner, C. Voegele, and Peter B. Robinson, "The Entrepreneurial Consumer," in *Research at the Marketing Interface*, ed. Gerald E. Hills, Raymond W. LaForge, and B. J. Parker (Chicago: University of Illinois at Chicago, 1989), 175–184.

4. Thomas P. Bergman, *The Essential Guide to Web Strategy for Entrepreneurs* (Upper Saddle River, NJ: Prentice-Hall PTR, 2001).

5. Tim P. Beane and Daniel. M. Ennis, "Marketing Segmentation: A Review," *European Journal of Marketing* 21, no. 5 (1987): 20–42.

6. Thomas V. Bonoma and Benson P. Shapiro, *Segmenting the Industrial Market* (Lexington, MA; Lexington Books, 1983).

7. Gerald E. Hills, "Market Analysis and Marketing in New Ventures: Venture Capitalists' Perceptions," in *Frontiers of Entrepreneurship Research*, ed. K. Vesper (Wellesley, MA: Babson College, 1984).

8. Bonoma and Shapiro, *Segmenting the Industrial Market.*

PART IV

INTERNAL STRUCTURES AND PROCESSES

Eight

Developing Internal Processes— Operations, Pricing, and Finance

In the earlier chapters we have been looking externally at the world. In this chapter we turn internally to focus on developing capabilities related to critical internal functions: operations, pricing, and finance. Developing the management team to handle these processes is also part of internal processes—a very important one—and therefore another chapter is devoted to it. Internal processes represent the resources and capabilities of the firm to address the external world. We are focusing on those that are necessary for delivering the product(s) or service(s), and those that will need to be developed or acquired to ensure the success of the venture. In fact, there is even the Malcolm Baldrige Award for small firms that show exceptional skills at operational performance.[1]

Operations include manufacturing, distribution, and information systems. Information systems together with finances also form the control system of the firm. Internal processes ensure that the firm can deliver on its promises; therefore building sound and functional business operations are critical, although it is sometimes difficult to pass the costs of inefficiencies on to the customers. The days of cost plus pricing or guaranteed profitability are over. Operations are driven by costs and desired quality (in product and service). Needless to say, there will be multiple times when it is necessary to make trade-offs between controlling costs and improving quality. Building a functional operating plan will help explore ways to accomplish both. For example, certain tasks may be outsourced or automated. A general rule of thumb has however been to keep internally the firm's core competencies, although contrary ideas have been offered recently.[2]

Critical to internal processes is quality management. This has sometimes been described as total quality management (TQM). Originally developed for Japanese manufacturers, this view of building processes that are to achieve the highest levels requires that processes be managed. TQM has five major aspects:

1. management commitment to constant improvement of processes
2. leadership to make these processes work
3. customer focus, as they are the ultimate test of any successful process
4. total participation of everyone in the firm
5. constant process design, analysis, and improvement

OPERATIONS AND OPERATIONS PLANS

Operations are the processes through which resource inputs such as raw materials, parts, creative talent, human resource capital (Chapter 9), selling skills, and a convenient location are converted to useful outputs that are to be sold to the customer as a valued outcome. In essence, operations determine *how* the company creates value for its customers. Therefore, leaving this to chance or totally outsourced to others is neither a viable nor a prudent option. Operating plans describe the control procedures and flow of activities required to provide services or products and any associated activities within the firm. In an operational plan for a new venture, the following issues should be considered:

- Identify the firm's specific location(s) and reason for such location(s).
- Develop operating policies and procedures.
- Describe operating facilities and layouts.
- Describe purchasing procedures.
- Describe distribution mechanisms and partners.
- Explain inventory management procedures.
- Establish quality control.
- Describe customer-service procedures.

An operations plan will give a detailed statement of how the proposed venture will work in reality. It is important to understand that such a statement is not merely for external stakeholders, but it is as much a blueprint or documentation of the processes for everyone involved in the venture. First and foremost, while writing such a plan it forces the entrepreneur to really think through key processes that need to be in place prior to opening the doors to customers. Engineers of information systems use flowcharts and documentation to describe a software program. They even use such flowcharts to show

how the software and hardware in a system are connected. An operations plan can be seen as the flowchart. It provides the documentation of all key tasks in a task system called *a firm*. It should show all the inputs and outputs, what resources are responsible for them, and when they occur within the overall process. Moreover, it will show the true complexity of operations and should also indicate where things can fall apart or have bottlenecks. Finally, it should be a road map for when the dream comes true and sales begin to soar. It should help the management in scaling-up operations in order to meet any increasing demand. It may sound strange, but true—never create a demand that cannot be met. Success can be as sweet as honey or lethal.

Operations are the internal processes and resources that create the *value*. It is the value created that distinguishes the firm from competitors, and it is the kind of value customers are prepared to pay for. Here it is important to understand that we mean *customer-perceived* value. What the entrepreneur thinks is value is not always perceived as valuable by customers. However, once the firm understands what its customers value, the operations plan will ensure that the internal processes enable this value to be created, hopefully in an efficient manner.

The key question then is "What resources are required to create value?" Value creation requires resources, but what are these? Knowing exactly where value is created enables the creation of unique advantages from the operational functions. For example, Southwest Airlines built a competitive advantage by using secondary airports (Dallas Love Field, Ft. Lauderdale-Hollywood, and Baltimore-Washington International Airports) and one type of aircraft (Boeing 737). This was a carefully thought-out intentional strategy and not just something that happened because they could not use the primary airports. The secondary airports were actually often closer to business centers than major hubs, and the cost of operations at these facilities was actually less than at the primary airports. Finally, never forget that various external factors influence operations. Again, for example, Southwest Airlines avoided northern states for years because of the delay factors due to weather in winter.

The above example of Southwest Airlines shows one critical element of value creation: location. Some may argue that location is not part of operations but marketing. However, location is critical to operations as it involves management of what is called the supply chain, and that refers to internal processes that reach externally. Where the business is located may be critical to the customer. For example, if you want to supply to Wal-Mart, you will need to have an office and operations in Bentonville, Arkansas. It is important for the entrepreneur to know all significant links in the supply chain from raw materials (or purchase from a manufacturer) to delivery of the finished product or service.

Harvard's Michael Porter introduced the concept of the value chain as a way of managing internal operations across the interface to the market.[3]

Even if the entrepreneur chooses to outsource certain parts of the firm's operations, it will be necessary to manage the suppliers. There is some evidence that as many as two-thirds of fast-growing firms outsource some part of their operations. One may outsource subassembly work, payroll administration, direct mailing, or advertising. Many small firms will outsource computer networking or even fulfillment and shipping and handling of goods. The simple reason for these decisions is that to do it yourself costs too much and by going outside one gains economies of scale that only a larger operation, focusing on these processes, can achieve and pass on to its customers. However, we do not recommend outsourcing that are supposed to be the core competencies of the firm.

Another internal process area is the management of inventory and purchasing. An effective strategy here requires identifying who buys and what their budget limitations are. It is necessary to identify specific procedures to follow, to assure that goods are bought, paid for, and accounted for. One needs to learn to screen potential vendors to assure an adequate flow of raw materials and services. There are also ethical issues related to purchasing, such as taking gifts from suppliers, conflict-of-interest issues, and what purchasing information is confidential. Failure to adequately control inventory can cost sales or tie up too much of the firm's capital resources.

Managing inventory is perhaps one of the areas where most new or small firms are most inefficient. Unless the firm is a service business, most firms will have some inventory that needs to be managed. Processes that need to be managed here include the cost of financing to purchase inventory, the costs associated with storage of inventory, insuring inventory, inventory lost due to theft or damage, and what happens when the inventory is old and obsolete. It is necessary to find methods for tracking inventory. One knows that there are inventory problems if inventories are growing faster than sales, or obsolete inventory is written off. Additional problems occur if there is insufficient inventory, and customer complaints about back orders and missed deliveries or increasing lead times occur.

Checklist on Operations

As in previous chapters, responding to the checklist below is not to be considered a sufficient development of an operational plan, but rather a set of questions that when relevant need to be addressed.

1. Explain the process that will be used in receiving orders for the product or service.
   a. Be specific about key tasks.
   b. Diagram key systems using flowcharts.

2. Explain key administrative policies, procedures, and controls.

   a. Billing the customer

   b. Paying the suppliers

   c. Collecting the accounts receivables

   d. Reporting to management

   e. Providing for training, promotions, incentives, and so on

   f. Establishing inventory control

   g. Handling warranties and returns

   h. Monitoring budget control, travel, phone usage, suppliers, car allowances, and so on

3. Create a flowchart of information and key tasks throughout the system.

   a. Identify all the things that should happen in a transaction.

4. What documents and databases are needed for a transaction?

   a. Invoice, sales tickets, charge documents, e-commerce databases, and so on

5. How is the product made, is the firm differentiated from competitors based on operations or distribution?

6. Has it been described in detail how customers get the product or service?

   a. What is the distribution chain?

   b. Why are distributors willing to carry the product or service?

7. When will the product or service be ready?

8. What documentation is available for the product or service?

PRICING AS OPERATIONS

Internal operations are reflected in the pricing strategy the venture is capable of implementing. When developing a pricing strategy it is important to remember that customers value what they pay for; hence, all payments should be justified in the customer's perception of important benefits. Most customers—individuals or firms—have a need to preserve their sense of self-control by having a choice, which comes through competition. However, it is not always the final costs that determine a purchase decision by a customer. One central issue can be the terms given for making a purchase. Does it include a quality product and after-purchase service? What are the impacts of these on the profit margin? Does the customer have a preference for pre- or postpayment. For certain services (like vacations) people prefer to pay in advance. For some products people prefer to pay postdelivery (like a new car). Moreover, every entrepreneur needs to consider issues like discounts, coupons, frequent user discounts, and so on to attract customers to their product or service. However, it is important to know that it is very hard to lift prices; that is, it can be dangerous to start out with low prices or discounts that are likely to jeopardize the profitability of the firm. A newly starting firm rarely has enough funds, and to deliberately cut prices as the loss of earnings can be fatal for a starting firm. Remember all pricing strategies are here to achieve: increased sales, increased market share, maximized cash flow, increased profits, creating barriers to competition, more defined image of the firm and product, and finally control over demand.

Another way to look at pricing is by the strategies that can be employed. These fall into four fundamental types.[4] These are new-product pricing, competitive pricing, product-line pricing, and cost-based pricing. Within each of these are substrategies with particular foci. For example, within new-product pricing one can price skim, that is enter at a higher price until competition forces a reduction. In this strategy the initial higher price allows for the reimbursement of development costs. Another substrategy is penetration pricing, where the firm wants quick acceptance of their product and broad distribution. This is especially useful when there is a highly competitive market. Here the hope is that with increasing market share one recoups costs. This is a gamble we do not often recommend for new firms. Another approach to new-product pricing is what is called experience-curve pricing. This occurs often in technology products where one begins with a high price, and as technology helps one reduce costs the firm can reduce price. Remember, it is easier to lower prices than to raise them. In this way the firm can have advantage over competition by taking control of the price for a product in the marketplace. When thinking of competitive pricing strategies, there are leadership pricing (the firm initiates price changes for the industry), parity pricing (the price is based on what the competition is pricing and puts theirs in line with the industry standard), and low-price supplier (this is pricing below costs to attract customers to other products that are in the firm's portfolio). Think of this as "milk" as the low-price teaser that will draw customers into the store to buy expensive meats or other grocery goods.

The next major set of pricing strategies is built around product-line pricing. One can adopt complementary product pricing, where the core product is priced low because associated accessories or supplies have high profit margins. Think of razors and razor blades or printers and ink cartridges. A related strategy is price bundling, where a product is bundled with several others and the sum of the costs is less than the total of individual products. Microsoft Office suite of software is one such example. Another product-line approach is called customer-value pricing. Here products are modified to meet different customer groups and their needs and the price are adjusted accordingly.

Finally there is cost-based pricing, which used to be true in military purchases of aircraft, for example. This was for many years the most widely used
strategy, but it has significant weaknesses as this approach ignores the market
demand and what customers are willing to pay. To do cost-plus pricing
requires actually knowing what are the true costs of producing a product or
service. This should include the actual costs of running the business and a
profit margin to arrive at the set price. Sometimes this strategy is called markup pricing or rate-of-return pricing.

Pricing Checklist

As mentioned before, responding to any of the checklists is not sufficient
effort at the development of a pricing strategy, but rather to get one to ask
questions about one's pricing.

1. What are the three biggest objections potential customers would have about your
   product and is price associated with these?
2. Design a pricing sheet for customers.
   a. Show purchase price, quantity discounts, shipping procedures, billing procedures, warranties, and maintenance contracts.
3. Compare the pricing strategy to that of the competition.
   a. Volume discounts, discount pricing, and premium pricing.
4. What are the policies on negotiating a price for large orders or on special price
   deals for penetrating the market?
   a. Quantity discounts, introductory offers, and so on.
5. Do people have to buy other services from in order to use the product?
6. Describe the pricing procedure for the industry.
   a. How do they differ? If yes, explain why.
   b. What are traditional markup and discount structures?
7. If the business is importing or exporting the product, what are the costs and procedures that must be added?
   a. Taxes, tariffs, foreign exchange of dollars, import/export broker, and so on.
8. Show the prices of all products minus their direct costs so that the reader can
   quickly grasp their profit potentials.
   a. Put this in chart form.
   b. Are any special offers made?

FINANCIAL CAPITAL AND SOURCES

Now we want to turn to one of the most important of the internal processes
every entrepreneur must master. It is quite often the case that people think

money is the greatest concern of entrepreneurs. Yes, money is important. But it is not more important than the business concept. The business concept will tell why money is needed and how much is needed. Money should be seen as the gasoline to operate the car. No car, then obviously no gas will be needed. In most cases, a smaller car requires less gas than is needed for an SUV.

A recent study across more than thirty countries[5] showed that an average of US$53,673 is needed to start a business. Again, this amount is dependent on the type of business. The amount needed to start a business is highest (US$76,263) in the business services sector and lowest (US$39,594) in the consumer-oriented sector. Obviously, the businesses that need the most start-up capital were those started with the intent to grow and hire employees. The study shows that firms that expect to employ ten or more persons five years after they open require an average of US$112,943 of start-up capital. However, as pointed out by Aldrich and Martinez,[6] most firms start small and remain small and they do not need more than US$5,000 on average to start.

When discussing the required means of financing it is important to realize that there are significant ways to reduce the amount needed by controlling costs and designing operations in an increasingly cost-efficient manner. Like in pricing, one cannot determine what one should be charging if one does not know what it will cost. Likewise one needs to know costs to determine what is needed to be raised to pay for those costs. In the remainder of this chapter we cover a variety of issues around revenue models as well as the development of financial models and key measures that investors are looking for from new ventures. It is important to understand how angel investors and venture capitalists make funding decisions. Also, in reality, bank lending to new entrepreneurial ventures is not easy even when available. The ugly part is that banks are asset-based lenders and they view start-up ventures as highly risky despite the realities of Enron and World-Com. Just remember that a bank is a place that will lend money if one can prove that it *really is not needed*. Be prepared to bet the spouse, your children, and your home if you go for bank lending as a new firm. Banks (and most formal investors) will expect not only a business plan, but also a personal guarantee. Remember, there are multiple sources of money and you may need to tap several of these typical sources at the same time:

- commercial loans from banks
- angel investors
- venture capitalists
- credit cards
- accounts receivable (supplier financing)

- equipment sales and re-lease
- advances on credit-card receipts
- initial public offerings (IPO)
- home equity loans
- governmental loan guarantee programs

In this section we also want to reveal several of the key internal processes that need to be mastered: the fundamentals of building pro-forma financial statements as well as the development of cash flows that reflect the various aspects of developing a business plan. If you are successful at raising funds, terms will have to be negotiated. Therefore, you have to learn how to read deal and term sheets. As in other chapters, we provide you the "checklist" for the financial section of the business plan. It is necessary to try to be as realistic as possible about the financial forecasts. This requires detailed knowledge of all the internal operations as well as the marketing costs. There is no such thing as "conservative cash-flow" projections. They are all "closet liberals." We have heard many a venture capitalist and angel investor say, "I don't believe a firm's cash or financial forecasts, as none are realistic, so it is important to believe in the people running the firm."

CRITICAL ISSUES IN ENTREPRENEURIAL FINANCE

The biggest issue from the standpoint of entrepreneurial finance is the creation of value for shareholders (investors, management), customers, and employees. Remember that without the "gas" of money the "car" of the firm will not go anywhere. When thinking of how to finance the venture, one needs to think of how the "value pipe" is sliced. Everyone, from management to the money guys, should be trying to assure that there is a mutually agreeable allocation of risks and returns. Remember that people are investing not just cash but also time into the venture. However, there have to be ways of covering the risks associated with cash, especially. If funds have been provided by debt, the financers can take control (think of the legal structures discussed earlier), or if an equity investment, they may stage their investment commitments to reduce their exposure. Remember that investors are looking for a

- good return on their investment
- fit between their expertise and the firm
- detailed and realistic financial plan
- detailed analysis of potential exit strategies (for them) within five to seven years
- firm that has a unique value proposition, not just another "me too" venture

FINANCIAL STRATEGY FRAMEWORK

It is important that the financial strategy fit, and be consistent with, the overall strategy of the new firm. A fast growth strategy requires a fast growth funding plan. Remember that the opportunity is what drives the business strategy (including marketing, operations, and management that create value). The business strategy drives the financial requirements that are based on operating needs and asset requirements. This is where having an understanding of the internal processes of the firm is critical as discussed earlier. The financial requirements will then drive the sources of financing and the deal structures (including debt, equity, and grants). When all these are together, the entrepreneur should have a financial strategy. This strategy will have limited degrees of freedom as to what can manipulate and change. The limits are often associated with future alternatives for funding, issues of risk and reward, and personal concerns of the entrepreneur and those of other investors.

One of the critical parts of the financial strategy process is to determine the cash-needs assessment of the firm. That is, it is necessary to determine how much capital it will take to start the new venture and to keep it running until the firm is capable of generating sufficient positive cash flow from revenues. This is neither an easy nor a totally accurate process. One's estimates of how long something will take or how much money it will take to achieve something are often very different from what actually happens. While one can benchmark against other firms based on public information, what is often difficult to acquire is the reality of what goes on inside the competition. Cash-needs assessments are best done systematically and tie back to other internal processes that you will need to have thought through.

There are essentially seven steps for doing a good assessment of cash needs. The first is to have done a process flowchart of the critical activities in the firm as discussed above. Then, it is necessary to identify the position that the firm occupies in the overall value chain for the customer and what to charge for the value that has been created. This is where the pricing strategy comes into play. Next, the time line for the business that includes how long it takes to turn investment cash into revenue cash will have to be developed. Are there seasonal factors (like all sales are at Christmas)? How fast can new customers be acquired? What does it cost? The next step is to develop the financial premises in terms of how the costs of the operations and revenues have been tied to the sales forecast (a critical part of the marketing plan). Remember that the estimates are most likely going to be wildly optimistic and it is important to learn to control one's "over confidence," as it will rarely be justified. The next step is the forecast of sales and your capital expenditures will have to be expanded. You rarely see a business plan that says it is going to lose money for as long as they actually do. It is often best to forecast sales in a way that may be helpful for determining what capital expenditures will be needed to make to support sales estimates. Once again, care and attention to detail will be fruitful here.

Once these steps have been completed it is possible to determine the capital requirements for the start-up. Employee training, leases, licenses, as well as equipment should be included. Many entrepreneurs forget soft costs like required deposits or setup fees. Finally, a sensitivity analysis should be carried out. That is, what happens if sales do not meet the estimates or the costs are significantly higher than anticipated? We always recommend a contingency factor, because the unexpected will occur. Who could have anticipated the 9/11 disaster in 2001, or oil price increases of over 100 percent in a year in 2006?

MONEY AND CAPITAL

Once the amount of needed cash has been determined it is possible to start thinking of where to acquire such funds. Fundamentally, there are five sources of capital: from internal operations, short-term debt financing, liquidation of assets, long-term debt financing, and equity financing. We will examine each of these in some detail. Short-term sources of debt financing include friends and relatives, accruals, trade credits, leasing, bank lines of credit, and asset-based lending (including pledging receivables, factoring, and pledging inventory). Long-term sources of debt financing include long-term bonds (callable and sinking funds), mortgage bonds, debentures, subordinated debentures, convertible debentures, debentures with warrants, income bonds, zero coupon bonds, indexed bonds, development bonds, pollution control bonds, and junk bonds. To be frank, few entrepreneurs see very much of these long-term alternatives until the venture is further in its life cycle. When looking at sources of equity financing there are a variety of issues that will have to be considered, such as preferred stock versus common stock, cumulative features, voting rights provision (do they have or do they not), and is this stock participating (management) or not? Remember this is part of developing the financial strategy.

It is important to remember that one of the single biggest sources of finance for a new venture is personal savings (and increasingly personal credit-card debt against home equity lines in the United States). Only about 40 percent of new firms are funded by a single source. Most have multiple sources and this is where institutional lenders will join the venture if they think the entrepreneur has "a skin in the game," in other words the entrepreneur's own money. It is nice to wish to use other people's money (OPM), but the reality is that the entrepreneur will have to put up more than just "sweat equity" from his or her personal labor. Investors are going to want to know whether the entrepreneur has money, even if relatively little needs to be invested in the business.

Debt Financing

Additional sources of debt financing include advance payments and deposits from customers, family and friends (be careful there are emotional costs here), professional advisors and acquaintances, "angels," private placement finders and packagers (be careful they sometimes promise the world but deliver little), present or potential customers, suppliers, past employers, prospective employees, Small Business Innovation Research (SBIR) grant program, strategic alliances, various state and federal programs, Employee Stock Ownership Plans (ESOPs), franchisees, licensees, and finally barter arrangements. It is important to check that there are no legal issues involved in this, such as when selling a security. Each of these debt approaches has its own strengths and problems, so pick carefully. Preferably use external advisors.

Bank Ability

Banks are basically asset-based lenders. In Australia, for example, if the person seeking a loan does not own physical property (land), it is very hard to get a bank loan for a venture. Remember banks want a security or asset. These can include accounts receivable, inventory, equipment, mortgage, conditional sales contract, and plant improvements. But, it is rare for banks to provide a loan up to 100 percent of the value of the asset. Most likely the bank will consider the credit capacity of the firm. We recommend you build a history with a bank of taking small loans and paying them off before you go in and ask for bigger amounts. They want to know your credit history.

Venture Capital

In reality, few new ventures are venture capital deals and even fewer will get venture capital (VC). If there are 300,000 new ventures a year, less than 1000 will achieve venture-capital funding. But, it is important to understand what venture capitalists are looking for. Any private investor, to some degree, if they have any sophistication, will be looking for the same thing. Here is a list in descending order of importance for VCs:

1. Capable of sustained effort
2. Thoroughly familiar with market
3. At least ten times return in five to ten years

4. Demonstrated leadership in the past

5. Evaluates and reacts well to risk

6. Investment can be made liquid

7. Significant market growth

8. Track record relevant to venture

9. Articulates venture well

10. Proprietary protection

FOUR KINDS OF MONEY

Fundamentally, there are four "types" of money: (1) money needed for operating the business, (2) money that is restricted, (3) money invested by the entrepreneur, and (4) potential money. We will go through each of these as we feel any entrepreneur needs to learn some lessons about each. *Operating money* is the money needed to meet payroll, pay taxes, pay-operating expenses, and make upcoming debt-reduction payments, that is, as the name says, to run the venture. The entrepreneur has to find ways to maximize income on money held for a short time. *Restricted money* is not readily available for *use* as it is dedicated to something else such as escrow funds, collateral for credit, pension or retirement funds (using these for something other than intended will send the entrepreneur into jail in most countries), time deposits, and insurance cash value. However, it may be possible to use restricted money to secure lower interest rates with a bank if they are the holders of the restricted money.

Invested money is money already "put to work," such as inventory, business real estate, stocks, bonds and other securities, and some types of insurance. We do know that the value of many small firms depends on their real-estate holdings rather than the value of the firm itself. Therefore it is advisable to balance risk and return by spreading the investment among various types of invested money. *Potential money* can, for many, be the most important form as the entrepreneur can impact the form. Potential money can be seen as accounts receivable, the credit value of customer goodwill, all contracts for future goods/services, the current inventory's value, and obviously the value of business property and equipment.

It is important to look for more efficient ways to turn potential money into real money. The aim is to shorten the time from spending the cash to making a product/service and receiving cash for the service or product. This is what is meant by the "timing of turning cash into cash." There are five ways to turn potential money into real money by improving cash flow: bill it sooner; collect it sooner; pay it later; negotiate volume and early pay discounts; encourage large orders. All these assume that the operations will support these approaches.

THE VALUE OF BOOTSTRAP FINANCING

The harsh reality about financing a new venture is that only people who either "love you" or "love your idea" will give you money. The "real way" to finance the start-up firm without outside investment is known as "Bootstrapping." This is growing the firm with self-generated funds the firm produces through normal operations. Bootstrapping is important not only because start-up investment is difficult to obtain, but also because once it is operational it is actually easier to get investment as the firm is then an established business. Many think the value of bootstrapping is also strategic. It keeps the entrepreneur focused on what is important about the business and very close to the customers. It also forces the entrepreneur to work closely with the vendors and helps minimize financial risk. It will also help the entrepreneur to keep more, if not all, of the company.

If there is a worry about "vulture capitalists" then bootstrapping is the best alternative. There is evidence that many dot-coms or e-businesses that started via bootstrapping are still operational while many of those who took VC monies have died out or been absorbed by others. Bootstrapping makes the company much more resilient and resourceful in the long run. Effective bootstrapping takes creativity, vision, and excellent selling skills, not only with customers, but also with vendors. Bootstrapping will also create excellent cash-flow management skills. It will force the entrepreneur to be innovative about how to do things, and it makes the entrepreneur more sensitive to cost issues.

Many entrepreneurs consider bootstrapping the *only* real form of entrepreneurship.

By incorporating as much bootstrapping into the business plan and financial plan, the venture will usually be a much better investment. The key to bootstrapping success is that it helps minimize most operating and financial risks in the business. There are seven creative ways that can be used to reduce the investment necessary for the business:

1. Prepaid deposits from customers
2. Using customer's money to make/buy goods
3. Negotiating vendor credit terms (remember most start-ups pay C.O.D.)
4. Negotiating extended terms
5. Barter
6. Making *all* costs variable
7. Strategic alliances with another firm for marketing

Every entrepreneur needs to understand their financial projects, and their business plan's financial section should contain some numbers. Too many entrepreneurs have someone else develop their financials, and they do not know what the numbers mean or how they tie to the various other parts of the plan (operations, marketing, etc.). Numbers should appear mainly in the form of a business model that shows the key drivers of the venture's success or failure. For example, in a manufacturing venture this might be the yield on a production process. For a publishing venture it might be anticipated renewal rates, while for software it might be the impact of various distribution models. Any used model should address the break-even issue. Break-even refers to the level of sales (and how many units) when the venture begins to make a profit. It is necessary to predict when the cash flow should turn positive.

BREAK-EVEN ANALYSIS

Earlier we mentioned that an entrepreneur needs to do sensitivity analyses. They also need to do a break-even analysis. This analysis (1) provides a "reality check" that can potentially save considerable time if the project is not feasible and (2) will provide the additional insight into the elements of a profitable idea. The processes involved are discussed below:

1. Estimate fixed cost. These are not necessarily start-up costs. These are costs that are independent of output. Examples include rent, utilities, and payments on equipment. Their periods should match (they should all be monthly, weekly, or annual).
2. Estimate variable costs expressed on a per unit basis.
3. Calculate break-even.
4. Calculate the associated market share.
5. Determine whether this market share is reasonable.

In other words, list the fixed costs (FC) (weekly, monthly, or annual) associated with your providing product or service. What is the sum of all these costs? List all the variable costs (per unit) associated with the product or service, and what is the sum of all these costs? Calculate break-even (FC/[Price − VC]). How large is the market for the product or service (preferably in units, not dollars)? Calculate break-even market share. Finally, is this market share reasonably attainable given the established marketing strategy that has developed?

FINANCIAL MODELS AND PLAN

The structure of the financial plan depends on its purpose. For a typical financial model requested by a bank, a one- to three-year financial projection should be completed. For a formal business plan, this projection should be supplemented by three- to five-year historical financial statements (if available). It is not sufficient to include photocopies of these statements in an appendix, if the firm already exists. They should be restated in a format similar to that of the projections. The entrepreneur should be actively involved in developing the financial model for the venture. It is an involved, but essential and valuable, process. The following steps, which build on the cash-needs assessment, are helpful, but alterations may be required depending on the financial mechanism of the business and the industrial segment.

Step 1: Project Sales. Business-plan market research should be completed first. Use revenue drivers as much as possible (product units or service customers for example). Keep variables on a single worksheet so you can easily alter the assumptions in order to test various scenarios. Reference the resultant dollar revenues on the Income Statement.

Step 2: Estimate Cost of Goods (COGS). Fill in COGS drivers on the worksheet (dollar per unit or dollar per customer, for example). Then reference the dollar COGS on the Income Statement.

Step 3: Estimate Collection Time. Estimate collection characteristics using days in receivable or percent collected (i.e., 20 percent collected after one month, 40 percent collected after two months, etc.). Reference the resultant accounts receivable values on the balance sheet.

Step 4: Estimate Inventory Requirements. This should be based on future sales, not on current month's sales, for two reasons: (1) a growing company's inventory requirements will be extremely sensitive to sales growth and (2) small companies are particularly sensitive to cash flow, so working capital requirements should be as accurate as possible. Include all variables on the worksheet. Reference dollar values on the balance sheet.

Step 5: Estimate Overhead. List all overhead items on the worksheet and enter in estimates. Base them on sales or revenue drivers where appropriate. Reference the dollar figures on the Income Statement with an appropriate level of detail.

Step 6: Estimate Cash Requirements. Base the cash requirements on future sales. Cash/Sales figures can be inserted directly into the balance sheet.

Step 7: Estimate Start-up Costs. List the necessary start-up items on the worksheet. Insert the new purchase figures into the worksheet under each month. Estimate depreciation and reference on the Income Statement.

Step 8: Estimate Debt and Debt Payments. Insert variables "Debt" and "Interest Rate" into the worksheet. Reference this onto a debt amortization table, usually placed under the balance sheet. Project principal and interest payments. Reference interest payments on the Income Statement.

Step 9: Calculate Taxes Payable. Enter the estimated tax rate on the worksheet. Use this to calculate taxes on the Income Statement. Reference the first month's taxes payable on the balance sheet under taxes payable. If working on an electronic spreadsheet, set the cell for month two equal to the cell for month one plus the taxes from the Income Statement for month two. Drag this formula across the remaining taxes payable cells. Identify during which months taxes will be paid and adjust taxes payable for these months to the appropriate levels.

Step 10: Estimate Other Payables. Enter an estimate for days payable into the worksheet (more than one may be necessary). Use the multiple days payables to estimate accounts-payable-based inventory purchases. Do this by entering the appropriate equation into the balance sheet.

Step 11: Complete the Cash Flow Statement. Reference sales from the worksheet on the cash flow statement. Reference depreciation from the Income Statement. Reference changes in balance sheet accounts (accounts receivable, taxes payable, prepaid expenses, and accounts payable). Calculate cash flow.

Step 12: Test Assumptions. Adjust the assumptions about sales, costs, and so on, in order to test various scenarios. If this is a financial model, play with it for a week or two.

Step 13: Repeat Steps One through Twelve for Future Years. Complete projections ahead for an additional two to four years. Restate the previous year's year-end figures before each annual projection.

Step 14: Summarize. The full monthly projections should be presented for the first year. Quarterly projections should be provided for years one through three or five. Annual projections should also be provided for all years.

Checklist for the Financial Plan

As before, this checklist is to help the start of the process of generating critical financial information for a business plan.

1. Explain the assumptions made that form the basis for all the data contained in the financial statements:
   a. Sales
   b. Production
   c. Accounts Receivable and Accounts Payable
   d. Overhead Expenses
   e. Capital Expenditures and Depreciation
2. Prepare the following plans for the first-year budgets:
   a. Sales
   b. Production
   c. Operating Expenses
   d. Number and salaries of needed staff members
   e. Head Count Plan

f. Capital Expenditures

g. Start-up costs, fixtures, equipment, and so on

3. Prepare a cash flow until the business reaches cash break-even point or through the first year—by individual months. Some considerations are

   a. Start-up expenditures

   b. Accounts-payable procedures

   c. Accounts receivable

   d. Collection periods

4. Prepare the five-year cash flow using quarterly projections. Use a computer spreadsheet. Pitfall: Avoid using straight-line projections. Make sure to identify all business expenses.

5. Prepare Profit & Loss Statement for the first year.

6. Prepare a five-year Profit & Loss Statement:

   a. First year by quarter

   b. The remaining years annually

7. Prepare a balance sheet for each quarter for the first year of operation. Make realistic projections and coordinate with the Profit & Loss Statement.

8. Prepare a yearly balance sheet for the first five years of operation. Make realistic projections and coordinate with the Profit & Loss Statement.

9. Explain how the projections compare with industry norms. Are the costs, revenues, profits, and so on higher or lower than similar businesses?

NOTES

1. David A. Garvin, "How the Baldrige Award Really Works," *Harvard Business Review* 69 (1991): 80–93; Paul R. Stephens, James R. Evans, and C. H. Matthews, "Importance and Implementation of Baldrige Practices for Small Business," *Quality Management Journal* 12 (2005): 21.

2. Geoffrey A. Moore, *Dealing with Darwin: How Great Companies Innovate at Every Phase of Their Evolution* (New York: Portfolio, 2006).

3. Michael E. Porter, *Competitive Advantage* (New York: Free Press, 1985).

4. Peter M. Nobel and Thomas S. Gruca, "Industrial Pricing: Theory and Managerial Practice," *Marketing Science* 18 (1999): 438.

5. William D. Bygrave and Stephen A. Hunt, *GEM 2004 Financing Report*, www.gemconsortium.org (2005).

6. Howard E. Aldrich and Martha Argelia Martinez, "Many Are Called, but Few Are Chosen: An Evolutionary Perspective for the Study of Entrepreneurship," *Entrepreneurship Theory & Practice* 25 (2001): 41–56.

Nine

Management and Human Capital

Now we turn to issues of the management of the new venture and the differences between being a manager and being an entrepreneur. A digression at this point will be helpful. We have always believed that "form follows function." What we mean here is that mission, vision, and the business concept drive goals and objectives. It is goals and objectives that drive strategy, which in turn drives the structure and staffing of the venture. The issue here is to build a sound organization structure, apply extraordinary force, and coordinate and be concerned about timing. Organizations exist so that activities can be managed, people supported, and results achieved.[1] In this chapter we discuss what needs to be considered while structuring a venture and the processes of finding the right people. The trick is to be entrepreneurial in the management processes.

In 2006, *Fortune* had a lead article on how management rules and styles have changed since ten years ago.[2] The article compared the large firm management style of Jack Welch, former CEO of General Electric, with what many would describe as the "Entrepreneurial Style" of management. For example, the old rule was that big firms owned the market. Today, agility is seen as most important and being big can actually harm a firm. Another view that has changed is marketing, where being number one or number two in market share used to be the goal. Today, that has changed to finding a niche and dominating that and building that niche on something new. In the 1990s shareholders ruled (and this usually meant the larger shareholders). Today, the customer is king again for even the largest firms. Another change in management is the idea of being lean and mean. The push for Six Sigma was all the rage in the 1990s. The trouble with Six Sigma is that it fixes existing problems and does not allow for new ideas or approaches. It is innovation that is the handmaiden of entrepreneurship, which is what Peter F. Drucker said already in 1954. Welch was famous for his ranking of employees and going with the "A Team." While that might remain a useful idea, the lesson for today is to find people to hire that are as passionate about the business as the entrepreneur is. Finally, in the past the CEO had to be charismatic and dominating. Today, it is more the CEO who is courageous who leads his passionate team.

One of the authors cut his entrepreneurial teeth hiring the passionate and achievement-oriented 3000 employees for the first major airline after the airline business was deregulated: People Express Airlines. In the late 1970s and early 1980s he learned the hard way that it is easier to hire the right people as entrepreneurs than it is to fire the ones you wish you had not hired. We believe entrepreneurs need to pay special attention to hiring, outsourcing personnel, compensation, and employee-management motivation. We have also learned the importance of advisors and boards along with how to find critical support from your networks (as discussed in Chapter 2). These are all skills the starting entrepreneur will have to master on the path to success.

One of the most important things any entrepreneur has to do, especially if innovation is a needed core competency of the firm, is to keep innovation forthcoming from all those in the firm. For this, employees should possess: (1) creativity skills, (2) content expertise, and (3) motivation toward the task. The critical task now is to turn creativity into an inherent part of the firm's culture as well as of management practice. It is this creativity that feeds innovation. Innovation exists in the work environment and occurs when creative management is combined with necessary resources and the organization's motivation to innovate. However, creative people are not easy to manage.

ENTREPRENEURIAL TEAMS

An entrepreneur can rarely do it alone. Fast-growing firms require entrepreneurial teams. It is important for any entrepreneur to understand the characteristics of successful entrepreneurial teams. These teams have complimentary competencies, proven professional expertise, solid individual and group competence, a clear understanding of and agreement on worthwhile (organizational) goals and measurable objectives, and a commitment to the firm's strategic goals and objectives. In addition we have discovered they often have shared values, confidence in each other, and mutual trust. There is a genuine need for each member of the team, and they know the roles that the others play toward the success of the firm. To achieve this they have extensive intrateam information flows (communication) that are direct, prompt, dependable, accurate, and, most important, useable. The team operates using performance-based rewards, with an equitable compensation system that evaluates the team but rewards the individual. The entrepreneurial team has expanded networks of contacts and resources that the entire firm can call upon. Most importantly, the entire team has entrepreneurial attitudes and personalities and the intention to succeed as a team.

However as easy as it may sound to create the ideal entrepreneurial team, there are challenges such as developing commitment, mutual respect, and trust. Then there is the challenge of achieving and maintaining synergy as if maintaining any harmonious working relationships were easy. Whenever two or more humans get together, you need to avoid the negative consequences of conflicts while building a cohesive, goal-congruent culture for growth. At this point we are reminded of Abraham Lincoln, the American president during the Civil War, who was asked why he chose General US Grant to lead the union army. Lincoln's reply was essentially that individuals who have no vices have very few virtues. Cigar smoking and whiskey drinking may be vices, but winning wars was a virtue to Lincoln and the nation at that point. There is something to the view that "A team leaders" hire "A team players." One of the challenges in an organizational plan is how you are going to deal with the challenge of managing "A team players."

THE ORGANIZATION

It may come as a surprise that for some the most important part of the business plan is "Management Team/Organization Plan" as it is the section that will convince potential financers that there are the right people capable of turning the business concept into a successful reality. Mediocre managers cannot make a good idea successful, but good managers can make a mediocre idea successful. A key characteristic of a *good* management team is that it has fundamental principles by which they organize the venture.

However, not all firms start with a team, but merely the self-employed entrepreneur. Many, in fact, remain entrepreneurs *en solo* or hire only a few persons. As shown in Chapter 1 a majority of all firms employ less than five persons. Only 3 percent of all firms manage to grow to employ more than 100 persons.[3] Those entrepreneurs that manage to grow their organization are likely to go through different stages or organizational types. These are (1) individual, (2) team organization, (3) hierarchy of authority, and (4) complex hierarchy. In the third and fourth type, the organizing starts to resemble that of large organizations and the activities are often closer to managerial ones rather than entrepreneurial.

When an organization grows, it does not always require hiring a lot of new persons, although increased employment is what most people think of when referring to a firm's growth. A firm can grow in terms of profit without adding a massive amount of employees to the firm. This is, for example, possible if the firm relies on subcontractors. For a starting entrepreneur it is advisable to keep salary costs down and this can be done not only by using subcontractors, but also by paying on individual actions and outcomes. This is often the preferred form with, for example, the sales staff who might be paid on commission. At some point, tasks may grow in complexity so that a team effort is required. Already when the firm grows beyond twenty persons, it begins to require some kind of hierarchy of authority and the complexity of the hierarchy is likely to grow as the firm becomes really large. However, in the early stages most tasks will be carried out by the management team. It is important that the entrepreneur finds a form that best fits the chosen strategy. Although a small firm in the beginning will tend to give multiple areas of responsibility to the small number of employees, it is important to understand that one person can rarely be CEO, CFO, CTO, CIO, and COO at the same time and be expected to perform each area of responsibility very well.

For example, science-based biotechnology firms are often founded by top scientists, where everyone among the founders most likely would be the best CTO (Chief Technology Officer). However, many times the top scientist will have to become CEO, CFO (Chief Financial Officer), or COO (Chief Operating Officer), which are not the areas of their prior core competence.

Starting ventures differ with respect to management in other ways too. In most management textbooks different forms of organizational structures are presented, for example, functional organizations, line organizations, and matrix organizations. Very large organizations are often divided into strategic business units (SBU). Moreover, large organizations have different departments, that is, marketing department, sales department, human resource department, production, and the like with respective heads of departments often called vice presidents. However, small firms do not have departments for the simple reason that they do not need such structures. These become relevant when the firm grows and begins to need hierarchies of authorities.

For the entrepreneurial firm the more typical forms of organization are the matrix and the network (Chapter 2). In a matrix organization, functional groups like marketing and finance are crossed by projects. In a network structure the basic unit of design is the employee, rather than the specified job or task. Employees, either individually or in teams, contribute to multiple organizational tasks and can be reconfigured and recombined as the tasks of the organization change. Work groups in a network are organized into crosscutting teams that can be on the basis of task, geography, or customers. The relationships among work groups are governed more by the often-changing implicit and explicit requirements of common tasks than by the formal lines of authority that characterize other structures. Network structure can go across organizational borders so that two ventures collaborate.

This is often the case within science-based ventures where a firm and, for example, a university research unit collaborate on commercializing a scientific finding. Such collaboration is often said to be organized in entrepreneurial teams.

FINDING AND KEEPING PEOPLE

To simply put, it is much easier hiring people than firing people, yet it is the reality of most firms, and entrepreneurs too will face both phenomena. Every entrepreneur faces the issue of finding, hiring, and keeping good people on their team. Fundamental to these are how to attract the people who are needed. For starting firms the issues of compensation and qualities of work can be real challenges, but if particular skills are critical, it is essential to think of these issues already at the start. In the business plan it will be necessary to explain how skilled employees will be found and kept. Moreover, it is not just skills and exceptional talent or potential that drives the selection of good employees. It is very important that the person fits with the organizational spirit or the entrepreneurial team. Every entrepreneur starting a firm should consider how to create jobs that have motivational potential within the new venture. Jobs should have meaningfulness by requiring a variety of skills, and the meaning is part and parcel of the work itself. People want to think that their efforts make a difference to others. But it is not just the meaningfulness that is important. Most people want to feel they have the responsibility to make things happen and the autonomy to make decisions about how to carry out their work. If a starting firm does not have the possibilities to pay high salaries, the fact that they can offer a work environment that requires the employee to carry out multiple tasks and take multiple responsibilities may attract the right skills.

We recommend that the entrepreneur make it explicit to himself or herself and all others in the firm about how the company is going to be managed and organized. Most people have at least implicit models and sometimes very explicit ideas (or models) of how certain organizations should be designed and managed. It is therefore necessary to be explicit about it— particularly if it is different. It is also important to justify why this model was chosen.

When hiring, clear specifications of job qualifications, expected professional competencies, job-related skills, and experiences are needed. The entrepreneur can ask, "Why would anybody want to work in the company and for the entrepreneur?" With respect to how the firm is managed and organized, questions to ask are: How are people "controlled" or "directed" in the venture? What are the most important characteristics that are sought in new people? It is better to hire temporary workers until the right full-time employees can be found. While an entrepreneur can outsource hiring to a consultant or "head hunter," an alternative is to use your entrepreneurial network to identify key people. Other proven methods include advertising in newspapers and trade publications, recruiting at schools and universities, public employment offices, referrals from current employees, and even relying on temporary help services. Regardless of how you identify employees, we strongly recommend checking references and making sure that candidates actually have the skills they claim (via skills testing). Here is where thinking small and hiring slowly is an advantage.

Employees should identify with the new venture. Some would call this a "Commitment Model." This is where attachment is to the people in, or the culture of, the firm. If this is the kind of firm the entrepreneur wants, the selection should be "culture fit," and thus gain coordination through both culture and peer control. This type of firm is best described by the entrepreneur who would say, "I want to build the kind of venture where people would only leave when they retire." Sometimes in building technology-based firms the entrepreneur may want another type of identity. This occurs when there is an attachment to challenging tasks and the selection is based on their current competence. What is important here is that control is through peer pressure of other experts in the firm. An example of this would be when you hear an entrepreneur say, "We want to have teams of people who are turned on by difficult problems. We want an environment of individuals who are certainly performance driven, achievement oriented, and customer focused."

COMPENSATION ISSUES

When discussing compensation it is good to remember the psychological fundamentals of intrinsic and extrinsic rewards. Individuals are intrinsically motivated when they seek enjoyment, interest, satisfaction of curiosity, self-expression, or personal challenges in their work. Most entrepreneurs have been shown to be highly intrinsically motivated and so are entrepreneurial teams. This is found in the fact that they tolerate long hours, low initial pay, and the potential of failure. Intrinsic rewards are derived from the interest challenge and enjoyment of the task itself. Extrinsic rewards are an outside source that intends to control, or be perceived as controlling the initiation or performance of work. Individuals are extrinsically motivated when they engage in the work in order to obtain some goal that is apart from the work itself. Such rewards include recognition and compensation, such as money, stock, status, and other perks.

While every entrepreneur wishes in some way to never have to hire any-one, the reality is that if you are going to grow, you will ultimately need to hire and pay people. The functions of pay are both *external* (i.e., it is how you compete for talent against other people wanting to hire the same talent) and *internal* (i.e., maintaining labor, differential over occupations, motivate and align behavior, provide status, and finally provide a sense of equity in the organization). It is important to understand that there are certain market forces that need attention; that is, there are minimums that need to be met (not only minimum wage), but realize that there are compensation differentials across a country and between occupations. Therefore it is necessary to find information on current pay scales when in doubt.

Many entrepreneurs want to avoid labor unions, and the best way of avoiding them is by being a good employer. However, while this may work in the United States, there are many countries where unionization is very high (e.g., Finland and Sweden) and giving equity as part of compensation may be less easy; if nothing else, the tax authorities will want to have a say in that process. Therefore, it is essential to be aware of these traditions in a country. Some rules regulating labor are stated in the laws of the country, such as 2.5 days vacation for each month of the year, which makes twenty-five days paid summer vacation and six days winter vacation in Finland.

When developing the compensation packages, remember to avoid any perception of discrimination against any group. Build pay levels relative to the market and be clear what the basis for pay is. The composition of the pay package is essentially there to influence the ability to recruit and to reduce unwanted turnover. Pay is also one way to position the venture differently relative to the market. Benefits are critical to getting and keeping key people. The ability to offer benefits will influence the composition of the labor force, reduce turnover, impact hiring, and impact commitment to the firm. Generally, as firms grow the percentage of the pay, benefit package grows. As much as 25 percent of firms with under 100 employees offer some kind of benefit package. Some typical employee noncash benefits in the United States would include employee discounts, paid vacations and legal holidays, automobile expenses, travel expenses, housing support, moving expenses, work meals, recreational facilities, educational benefits, and finally pension (retirement) and health-care plans.

LEGAL ASPECTS OF HUMAN RESOURCES

While we have discussed the legal environment, in the area of human resources there are a number of laws you will need to be aware of certainly within the United States. There will be federal and state laws governing compensation, for example, the Equal Pay Act of 1963 in the United States. The entrepreneur is going to have to deal with a growing body of laws affecting safety in the workplace and compensation to injured workers. These are governed in the United States by the Occupational Safety and Health Act (OSHA) of 1970. Likewise there are laws governing liability for violating employee rights as well as discrimination against employees over age, race, and sex. Likewise there are laws governing family and medical leaves, and laws restricting religious bias. Perhaps among the most potentially damaging to an entrepreneurial firm are the laws and rulings governing sexual harassment. This includes, but is not limited to, verbal and nonverbal assaults of a sexual nature and physical harm. The entrepreneur can protect the firm from these lawsuits by being very careful about who is hired, keeping a detailed file on each employee (especially with respect to training and performance), always putting in writing any communications regarding performance, and finally before terminating any employee seeking legal counsel.

BOARDS OF ADVISORS AND DIRECTORS

Obviously, there are many types of firms and ventures ranging from public, private (or closely held), and family owned (can be private or public), to entrepreneurial (including private, family managed, and classic high growth). Most firms need a board, but entrepreneurial firms in particular need boards of advisors (business and technical) and as they raise significant funds, boards of directors. The role of boards is not just to control which is what many people think. Boards can be an extremely powerful resource of intellectual capital that a starting company would otherwise not be able to employ. Boards and advisory boards provide a broad perspective and a channel to discuss issues and problems of a CEO—who is quite often very alone with his or her issues and problems. If the members of the board are competent it will significantly help the entrepreneur attain the goals of the venture. Therefore, choosing the board members is not an easy task and not one merely to fill certain minimum requirements. Boards are also critical to resource mobilization and assistance (recall Chapter 2 on networks and the discussion on the strength of weak ties).

Organizational governance is one important role boards play. Advisory boards are just that: they advise, but it can be very dear advice. Their role is typically informal, having no legal standing, with no obligations to shareholders. The advantage with the advisory board is they can be easily assembled; they meet infrequently (around four times a year) with low time commitment on their part and minimal pay on the entrepreneur's part. The value of an advisory board is that it allows the entrepreneur to have some star names that will help in recruitment, sales, and/or investment. Advisory boards can be mentors because they can provide the experienced "gray hair." Advisory boards are also a source of funding.

Depending on the type of the firm the role of a board may at first be very informal, but in many countries a limited company requires a board with a president. As these regulations vary with country, it is necessary to check with the legal requirements. As a general rule, however, the number of individuals on the board should be an odd number and usually a board has three to five members. It is important to select board members that are willing to *work* for the firm, not just man a chair.

Boards of directors are legally required (as discussed in an earlier chapter). Boards can hire and fire CEOs, they have a strong obligation to all shareholders, and the potential for liability is there. Board members meet more often, usually eight to twelve times a year. For entrepreneurial boards their compensation is often in equity as they are spending time advancing the firm. As a firm matures, the board likewise will mature and will look more and more like that of a public corporation.

Boards enhance shareholder value. Their task is to select, evaluate, and compensate top management. One critical area boards ensure is management succession, especially in cases of crises. Boards help develop the positioning for the firm and metrics to monitor and critique strategic direction. Boards advise senior management by approving, monitoring, and reviewing appropriate policies. Many times they set the tone of the firm by creating a climate of full disclosure and by establishing ethical standards and legal behavior. Finally, boards monitor and critique operational and financial plans. The purpose of entrepreneurial boards is also to access potential investors, deal with the management of crises, provide a network of contacts, resolve conflicts among key players, and at times to even provide emotional support to the entrepreneur.

FINDING BOARD MEMBERS

The excuse for not having a good board is not that it is hard to find "good members." Finding good board members is essentially a sales process, where the entrepreneur sells the concept in combination with the perception of his or her own ability to succeed. The task is to make the venture attractive to them. Board members are looking for (1) investment opportunities, (2) relationships with other board members, (3) a window on areas of interest, (4) compensation, (5) recognition, (6) a challenging reciprocal learning experience, (7) impact on shareholder value, and sometimes (8) a vicarious feeling of *do it again.*

Finding the right people to be on your various boards is one of looking at personal characteristics. There are five characteristics to judge potential board members:

1. Integrity and accountability
2. Informed judgment
   a. Sufficient information
   b. Written
   c. Have expert input
3. Financial literacy
4. High performance standards
5. Communication sensitivity

When recruiting and retaining, the board aim high, cast a wide net, do extensive preselection interaction, and make sure there is "chemistry" among the board. Even if the potential members are known to the entrepreneur it is advisable to conduct reference checks and to have a written understanding of what is expected. Once the board members are chosen, they need to be educated about the firm by giving them the business plan and any other materials about the firm. Finally, the board should also be evaluated as to how well they are doing in their job as a board.

The ideal "Early Stage Board" will have three members including the founder and two strong, independent directors who command the respect of the founding team. The independent directors should have sufficient experience either as directors or with the industry, and they may well have an economic stake through stock options. They need to be able to walk the fine line between being the entrepreneur's close confidant and maintaining objectivity as a fiduciary for all shareholders. The board of directors should act in the best interest of the firm as a whole and maintain the confidence of the firm.

THE ORGANIZATIONAL PLAN

The purpose of a formal organizational plan is to ensure the implementation of the operational plan. Form (organization) follows function (strategy). The venture should be structured to allow it to pursue its particular chosen strategy and market. Essentially, the organization depends on how the operational plan will be executed and reflects the ways in which the firm will solve problems including informational needs as well as coordination of efforts across functions. It is the structure (and yes, you do need one) that provides workers with the information, coordination, and incentives needed to get what you want done, actually done. Small firms also need some kind of structure. Even in small firms what gets measured is what has been done. Therefore, a critical part of any organizational plan is how effectiveness in meeting objectives will be assessed.

An organizational plan is the management section of a business plan describing the overall structure of the organization as well as the people in it. It will show the number of reporting levels between those who are in the front lines and the CEO. Obviously a firm with five persons is not likely to have any levels at all, but will have areas of responsibilities for the employees. For an entrepreneur, the fewer the levels are the better as it often means reduced fixed costs. As the venture grows, it will eventually need to reorganize, especially when markets or product lines are added. As the firm changes, so does the strategy and most often also the organization and staff. An organizational plan should not create frustration among employees, but aim at inculcating in them a positive attitude toward the firm and their responsibilities. While there will certainly be employee turnover, the aim of the entrepreneur is to *build*, and one way of doing this is by constantly improving the human resources in the firm.

Management and Organizational Plan Checklist

As in the prior checklists at the end of each chapter, this is to help an entrepreneur think through what this section should contain in the business plan. Any reader of this section should be able to understand the strength of the executive team, the human resources enabling this venture to succeed, and how these resources are managed and allocated.

1. Describe the contribution of the entrepreneur or entrepreneurial team:
   a. experience
   b. talent
   c. money
   d. time involved in the business, and so on
2. List key management personnel, job descriptions, and experience; also include
   a. successful track records
   b. prior experience
   c. relevant training
3. Describe the compensation package for the entrepreneur and the management:
   a. salary
   b. benefits

   c. stock options

   d. bonuses, and so on

4. Describe any contracts with the management team:

   a. noncompete agreements

   b. buy-sell, and so on

   c. briefly describe the contracts and place detailed contracts in the appendix

5. Show how the management team determines strategic objectives.

6. Demonstrate the team's commitment to making the business work.

7. Demonstrate the team's history of acquiring necessary resources.

8. Demonstrate the ability to control the needed resources.

9. Describe the ability to manage complex interactions.

10. Show adequate rewards for participants.

11. Are individuals committed to your mission?

12. Are individuals in your firm working together toward an agreed-to set of goals?

13. Will your firm perform up to its potential?

14. Whether the section shows

   a. clear role differentiation through strategy-related job descriptions that specify responsibilities, authority, and accountability

   b. clear specification of job qualifications, expected professional competencies, job-related skills, and experiences

   c. that a broad search for best applicants was carried out

   d. clarified mutual expectations in advance

   e. incentives, appropriate rewards, and opport unities for advancement

NOTES

1. G. A. Michaelson, *Sun Tsu: The Art of War for Managers* (Alcoa, TN: Pressmark International, 2000).

2. Betsy Morris, "The New Rules," *Fortune*, July 11, 2006, 70–87.

3. Howard E. Aldrich and Martha Argelia Martinez, "Many Are Called, but Few Are Chosen: An Evolutionary Perspective for the Study of Entrepreneurship," *Entrepreneurship Theory & Practice* 25 (2001): 41–56.

PART V

SPECIAL ISSUES

Ten

Growth and Entrepreneurial
Family Firms

As firms become established, one moves beyond just the issues of opportunity recognition, planning, and initiating a venture into the fundamentals of growing a venture to the next level. Every entrepreneurial firm, even as it gets bigger, faces four big risks: strategic, financial, operational, and economic circumstances. *Strategic risk* emerges when the firm faces changes in its markets, new competitors, or shifts in technology. These risks also include issues around growth strategies. *Operational risks* come through exposure to poor systems and controls that need to grow and change as the firm grows. These include exposure to loss due to poor internal systems and controls. Lack of such controls can affect funding options and quality assurance. *Financial risks* include changes in interest rates (cost of capital for growth), exchange-rate changes, and even increases in oil prices. *Economic circumstances risk* includes all those issues around changes in supply and demand, natural disasters like hurricanes or earthquakes, economic recessions, and failure of one's suppliers.

In this chapter we focus on how to manage growing organizations, building effective entrepreneurial management teams, and how to manage change and respond to risks. Critical, we believe, is how to keep the entrepreneurial spirit alive in a larger organization or as the firm becomes a family-owned and -managed business. One of the best responses to risks is to continue to be innovative. The harsh reality is that management must change with the size, complexity, and diversity of the organization. Being entrepreneurial and innovative as you get bigger is harder. There is evidence in the United States that at around forty employees, the entrepreneur has to stop personal management and begin to delegate. In smaller nations, especially those in western Europe, this shift happens at around twenty employees. In smaller countries there is a tendency to be in export orientation more quickly than in the United States. That is, as you reach a certain size, you have foreign operations and are forced to build structures to deal with this shift in markets. These structures and policies, while good and appropriate, can also inhibit innovation.

MANAGING GROWTH

As mentioned in the prior chapter on internal processes, growing a business also takes cash, often a lot of it. Cash for growing a business should first come from operations (profits), but, if insufficient, it will have to come from additional investment or borrowing. If funds come from internal operations this is known as the Self Financed Growth Rate (SFGR). The SFGR is determined by how much cash a unit of sales gives off, how much cash this unit of sales growth requires, and how long this cash will be tied up before it comes back. Also for every dollar, yen, or euro you spend, what do you receive in revenues and over what period of time? Cash in a growing venture must be managed strategically taking into account both risk and return. Risk comes from innovation and the development of new products and services as your firm grows. Remember that entrepreneurial enterprises journey into the unknown where many factors can be considered, but not all are known and many are totally unanticipated. So always remember to have cash available for when you will really need it. In hindsight, what happened looks obvious once it has occurred. That is why it is said your venture will cost twice as much as you plan and take thrice as long, or vice versa.

Visionary leadership is needed for managing growth from the entrepreneur and the entire organization. Leadership here is focused on long-term strategic goals that extend throughout the venture. This leadership style is built on the culture created during the start-up phase. Entrepreneurial leadership in the growth phase of an organization also means recognizing and capturing new opportunities and undertaking constant innovation that become obvious as the firm gains additional capabilities. Remember that strategy changes as the firm grows. It may be implicit at first, but it will become more formalized and require formal communication later. This means that strategy is cooperatively developed with your growing management team. Growing firms may still use networks instead of staff to solve specific issues with operational, informational, financial, and special assistance, but more and more critical expertise will be available internally.

As your venture grows, seizing a new opportunity can be very good in and of itself. Growth forces you to learn new skills that will open the door to other opportunities that were previously unavailable to the enterprise. Successful entrepreneurship involves climbing the opportunity ladder by increasing the organization's capabilities as the firm deals with present opportunities that allow you to grab new opportunities that are made available. As your organizations grow larger, however, the method of operating changes. One can cooperate with other firms while competing with them as well as the firm grows. At this stage you might find yourself networked with competitors whom you call on when you get that order you are going to have trouble fulfilling. In addition, you need to put in additional structures, processes, and controls that produce a bureaucracy with set policies and procedures. The entrepreneurs, as they grow, need to minimize nonincome generating middle-level management, which is often the enemy of innovation and new opportunity development. You have to work on instilling and extending entrepreneurship, especially as you hire new people. An example of a larger firm that has maintained this entrepreneurial management style is 3M. Every year, despite the fact they are a global firm, they bring out a significant number of new products because they foster an innovative and entrepreneurial environment within the firm. With time and growth, you will have to rejuvenate the venture and rekindle innovation and entrepreneurship. Only entrepreneurial leadership's constant attention is the "force" that prevents the rise of unneeded bureaucracy or compliancy.

THE ENTREPRENEURIAL FAMILY FIRM

What many entrepreneurs fail to appreciate is that their firm often quietly morphs into a family-owned and -managed firm. One of the great strengths of family firms is a strong tradition of shared moral and ethical values. This is an area in which the family firm demonstrates the intersection of three social systems: management, ownership, and family. As the entrepreneurs grow older their personal goals change as do the firm's business goals. With these changes in goals, there are required changes in strategy. One of these changes is that entrepreneurs often have families, many of whose members will join the venture in some capacity. In many family businesses, the difference in goals between the generations (say, founder and offspring) becomes a major problem in family succession.[1] In many family firms, one will have to work on preserving and maintaining entrepreneurship as family firms get ossified at times and will not innovate. Growth is usually good. Larger organizations typically have more resources, greater credibility, and more employees beyond just family members. It is easier to be nimble and change with new knowledge and innovations when the firm is small, but as the venture grows, it becomes necessary to avoid the rigidity of status quo or the tyranny of common knowledge that often occurs in family firms.

ISSUES FACING FAMILY FIRMS

The reality is that entrepreneurs' personal goals over time may become less attached to the firm. They may want someone in the family to take over or consider exiting the firm to capture the wealth accumulated there. Likewise the assets needed or investment necessary for the firm to grow may be beyond what the entrepreneur considers personally acceptable or available. This may lead to the decision to consider selling. While this reduces the need for the family to provide management succession, it does create issues of wealth management and inheritance. The entrepreneur can sell to another family member, to management, and/or to others outside the firm. While it is not likely that most entrepreneurs will be involved in an Initial Public Offering (IPO), it does remain an option for some. Other options include liquidation or shrinking and regenerating the firm in a new direction to better fit the entrepreneur's personal goals.

There are a number of other issues that face a family-owned and -managed firm as it continues to develop. One is that families often grow faster than the size and value of the firm. Rapid growth of family size has a diluting effect on potential managerial control. It is also true that what holds a family together often changes from bonding by biological-emotional and emotional ties to more bonding legal ownership by the third generation. There is also the reality that the firm often becomes the "totem pole" around which the family "dances." That is, an individual's personal identity is equated with legal ownership of the family firm. As family takes on more and more managerial roles (entrepreneurs often want to take care of their children and other family members), there are increasing barriers to promoting non-family to top managerial roles where outside expertise is clearly needed. If one expects family members to join the firm, then there is the issue of educating family members for management positions and learning to treat them as employees, not family.

As the firm grows, the goals and objectives of the first generation may be very different from those of later generations (they do not realize the hard work it took to create the firm) and thus you see disgruntled shareholders, often minority shareholders, or individuals without the necessary skills and training to do their jobs within the firm properly. There is also the changing nature of relationships between family members as they age and take on new social roles. Likewise there are changing relationships with employees and family as the firm grows and the management becomes more distant from new employees. Entrepreneurs often find that some employees have not grown with the firm and have not kept pace with the needs of the firm. If building an effective management team was critical at the start-up stage, it remains critical as you grow a family-owned and -managed business. Male entrepreneurs often forget that the female members of their family can be strong managers. Part of this reluctance reflects the changing roles for men and women in various cultures and ethnic groups. One of the biggest issues that face family firms is the lack of strategic planning for both the family and the firm. We believe entrepreneurs do not just write a plan to start a firm, but they write one to take the family-owned firm to the next stage and to address changes in the environment.

A key to having a successful firm is to deal with the role of the family in the firm early and effectively. This will eliminate many of the less critical issues facing the firm in the future. We are not suggesting that family need not be involved, but that the entrepreneur plans this process as well. One way to do this is by focusing on goal setting for both the family and the family in the firm. Is every one headed the same direction? This is the reason you need individual "strategic" plans for families that are involved in the firm. It is very hard to have a functional family-owned and -managed business if the family is dysfunctional. To make the family firm successful it is important to understand the complexity of the family enterprise. Family firms are the basis of all economies, the most complex economic units, and the oldest historically. Increasingly for family firms to survive in the twenty-first century, there needs to be respect for different generations without either needing the approval of the other. Generational differences are increasingly becoming issues in family-owned and -managed firms worldwide.

For a family firm to outlast the first generation there is a need for a shared vision of the future of the family and the firm. Family-owned and -managed firms are the most complex because they have both the complexity of the business environment and the complexity of the family. Here once again leadership becomes critical. This leadership challenge is most obvious in dealing with the related issues of succession and inheritance. Inheritance is the transmission of property or wealth while succession is the transmission of a particular position in a firm. To deal with these there are in essence two sets of strategic decisions: eliminating personnel or potential leaders, and dividing existing or creating new assets. When one cannot find appropriate leadership through family succession, then there are the challenges of bringing in outside management and/or professionalizing family managers in the firm. Owners of family businesses traditionally resist bringing in outside managers or boards of directors because they do not want anyone telling them what to do or because they do not want to reveal company secrets. We believe entrepreneurs need to bring in outsiders in both management and the corporate board if the firm is going to have sufficient resources to grow.

One of the great management challenges of a family firm is avoiding the perils of conflict over roles, power, money, traditions, growth, and personalities.

This is *frequently* frustrating and often an unsuccessful juggling act. This is because family firms literally begin when the entrepreneur starts a firm and the family is involved in any way. The conflicts increase as the firm moves from the "owner-manager" to a "partnership of siblings" and finally to a "consortium of cousins." This transition of ownership is compounded by these changes in family over time.

The resulting three-dimensional model of family business (ownership, family, and business) makes the management of the family business the bookend to the complexity and challenge of starting the firm. Figure 10.1 shows just how complex family firms can be.

What we have attempted to do in the above discussion is to show the transitions the founding entrepreneur has to make. These concerns in the business arena move from the reliance on one person, to building management, to dealing with excessive attachment to the firm, then learning to let go, and finally successor development. In the arena of family the founding entrepreneur is dealing with attention to family, family resentment, building family competence, entry of in-laws, and sometimes team building among siblings.

FIGURE 10.1
Three-dimensional Model of Family Business

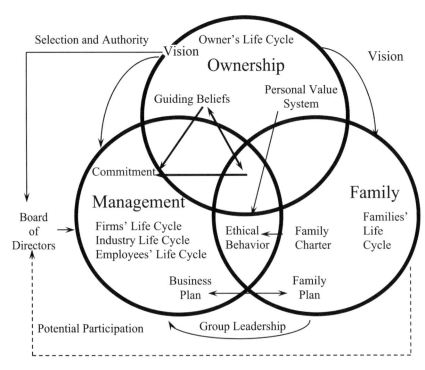

In the ownership arena the entrepreneur is obviously dealing with passing on control and choosing an appropriate ownership model. In all these realms the entrepreneur is the one who is leading the business or may involve a spouse in the leadership of the firm and family. In the family arena the postentrepreneurial family should be focused on building family competence, harmony, and teamwork. They must address historical roles and issues as well as a potentially growing difference in the cultures and backgrounds of the different family branches because of marriages of children and grandchildren. The family will have to manage issues of status and fairness as well as the acceptance of differences in family members and their personal goals and objectives including freedom of career choices. Communication in a multigenerational family is often difficult and frequently indirect. As the firm grows, issues in the ownership realm are around managing reinvestment and shareholder liquidity, and board representation. Governance in the immediate postfounder period is usually by the parents in the family or a family-controlled board. This will need to change with time and as the number of generations increase. In the generation after the founding entrepreneur, the family-owned and -managed firm is now dealing with:

1. building professional management and systems
2. escaping the founder's shadow
3. caretaking of the firm while recreating the "Founder's Dream"
4. redefining the leadership model
5. developing the next generation of family members to lead the firm

For the family firm, keeping the entrepreneurial spirit alive is hardest in the period of the "cousin consortium." Here the business issues are concerned with nonfamily leadership, aggressive reinvestment, and maintaining innovation. In the family arena, the concerns are managing family scale and the potential conflict between different branches of the family. If there is going to be long-term viability of the family-owned and -managed firm work, then there has to be a healthy relationship among siblings. There has to be a shared vision or dream about the family firm. This begins with the founding entrepreneur setting the vision. This requires a relatively similar approach or business philosophy. Individuals in the family and in the family firm must have the ability to capitalize on the unique talents of each person as well as their deep knowledge of a shared history of the firm. What is sometimes hard to keep in a family is the notion of a generosity of spirit or "one for all and all for one." Certainly there will be rivalry, but the issue is to make sure it is constructively managed, which certainly requires a sense of humor, if not patience.

MANAGING CHANGE

As the firm grows the entrepreneur is going to have to manage the change process. The reality is that there is nothing more difficult to do, nor more uncertain than trying to change an existing organization. The entrepreneur will need to manage change. That includes

1. what is being changed at the firm
2. the degree of change
3. the timing for change
4. the anticipated resistance
5. the size of the firm
6. how geographically spread out the firm is
7. the climate for change at the firm

Major changes in any existing organization are fragile and difficult to implement, especially in an entrepreneurial family firm. Even if entrepreneurs are familiar with the firm, it is still a good idea to do an assessment of the organization as it may be very different from what they think it is like, especially if it has grown. Remember it takes time, energy, resources, and skills for change to occur in even the most flexible organization. It is also important to remember that what to change is related to how one is going to change it. Constant communication is essential. It helps if the organization is committed to change, but the entrepreneur can overcome that with patience. One must manage the change process. It is essential that entrepreneurial leadership has a compelling vision of the future, which can serve as a new paradigm or a reframing of the existing situation in the firm. It is critical to know the goal of changing the organization.

DYNAMICS OF CHANGING ORGANIZATIONS

When we discussed family business it should have been clear that organizations are a collection of open systems. They expand, contract, and respond to various pressures. They are problematic at the best of times. All organizations are made up of the

1. Technical Task System
2. Social System
3. Managerial System
4. Political Arena
5. Organizational Culture

These are influenced by inputs (people, materials, and resources) and the environment external to the organization. Remember, trying to make changes in any of these systems causes the political system to be activated. Entrepreneurs must ask which of the three systems they are trying to change: the technical task system, the social system, or the managerial system. An entrepreneur learns that there is a relationship between strategy and structure of the organization. It is this alignment of systems and people that is the challenge of continuing entrepreneurial leadership.

The entrepreneurs trying to change their existing firm require that they not only assess if the external environment is stable and predictable or turbulent and unpredictable, but also the status of the internal climate of the firm. As for the management, they need to assess if it is formal and mechanistic or still organic and informal reflecting a newer firm. Next they need to assess the technical tasks to determine if they are certain and routine or uncertain and nonroutine. Assessing the firm's current culture is one of determining if it is nonadaptive and nonlearning or adaptive and learning. It is also important to know the kinds of employees the firm has and their personalities. Are they low in tolerance, externally controlled, and extrinsically motivated, or can you define them as having: high tolerance, self-control, and intrinsic motivation? All organizations, regardless of the people in them, are kept together by compliant behavior, identification behavior, and/or dedicated behavior. A good entrepreneurial family firm is hopefully held together by dedicated behavior more than by rules and policies.

Every organization resists change, even the most entrepreneurial. This is because human beings in general do not like to have to change when habits are formed. When the old way is comfortable and known, the entrepreneur needs to provide encouragement, support, but stay with the discomfort of the change if the employees are going to make the necessary changes. If the need for change is not clear or not accepted within the organization, then the entrepreneur needs to provide rational dialogue and participation in the process. The reality is that if there is continued resistance, this may require removal of those employees who cannot change, including family members. If the nature of the change is unknown or feared by employees, then the entrepreneur needs to educate, communicate, and make sure employees have active participation in the change process. It is also possible that as the organization grows, employees will need new skills. If this is the case, management must provide coaching, training, and the time to acquire new skills. At times, however, people wonder why the firm's leadership is trying to change employees' behaviors or why change is needed. The entrepreneur needs to provide clarification and acceptance through education, dialogue, participation, and incentives (including consequences). If there is no incentive to change, then the management needs to revamp the firm's performance appraisal and reward systems. Sometimes there is a lack of commitment to the change or resistance to the implementation of needed change. Effective leadership requires planning ahead for participation and involvement, and it will most likely require the development of a commitment plan. Sometimes, especially when merging firms, the entrepreneur will want to change the culture of the acquired organization. If the needed change is inconsistent with the current culture, then the management will need to change people's experiences. This can be achieved by means of paradigm shifts, reframing situations, education, and organizational development programs.

The social system in any venture is the most resistant to change (as one will learn in a family-owned and -managed firm). Change can threaten friendships and existing social patterns. While some people are always willing to change, 10 to 15 percent of people will never change. While it may be easy to get the 10 to 15 percent who are always willing to change, the challenge is to move the 70 percent in the middle. Remember that most people do not mind changing, as long as the management does not change them. Managing the change process requires dealing with the driving forces for change. Entrepreneurial leadership requires confronting the resisting forces against change and, finally, moving the organization to a new level. As for the entrepreneurs, they have to address the challenges of removing and reducing resisting forces while adding to and increasing driving forces for change.

CONCLUSIONS

In this chapter we have attempted to show how to use the fundamentals of opportunity recognition, planning, and initiating a venture into surmounting the trials of growing one. The issues of managing growing organizations, building effective entrepreneurial management teams, and the management of change are the ones every entrepreneur will face, but the earlier skills learned as an entrepreneur will help in this growth period as well. Be prepared for the challenge as the real issue is how to keep the entrepreneurial spirit alive in a larger organization.

NOTE

1. Kelin E. Gersick, John A. Davis, Miriam M. Hampton, and Ivan Lansberg, *Generation to Generation: Life Cycles of the Family Firm* (Boston: Harvard Business School Press, 1997); P. C. Rosenblatt, L. de Mik, R. M. Anderson, and P. A. Johnson, *The Family in Business* (San Francisco: Jossey Bass, 1985).

Appendix: Putting a Plan Together and Avoiding Pitfalls

In this section we want to shift to some practical discussion and applications to avoid doing the things that entrepreneurs do inadvertently to kill a good business concept. We want the reader to learn how to avoid those errors when talking to others about the new venture. As we have said earlier entrepreneurs need to tell, or show, others the value of their concept. As we have noted entrepreneurs will need outsiders to come to work for them, to invest in their venture, or to even be their customers. We have learned that packaging and presentation of a business and its related strategic business plan are as important as the plan or the venture concept itself. We believe every entrepreneur needs to spend the time on the front end on the firm's name and logo. Entrepreneurs are building a brand at the very start and need to remember that. All venture capitalists have watched great presentations of mediocre ideas save them and they have seen great ideas die because of a poorly written or presented plan. It is in the presentation that they really see if the entrepreneur can sell. Thus, how to package a venture is a critical skill to learn.

In this section, we provide an overview of the simple *dos* and *don'ts* in writing an effective business plan and presenting the business to others. At this point the reader should pull from the previous chapters the answers to the checklists and start to create a draft business plan. In this section we give some examples of the types of responses that a reader might have from reading any business plan. In addition, you will find below an example of a stand-alone executive summary. A key to being a good entrepreneur, whether selling a product/service or the firm to investors, is learning to craft a compelling story. It is the story of the venture that is the basis for a business plan. Effective presentation of the story is not a quick and easy process. Take the time to do this right. Finally, if the investors like the venture, they may offer a deal and term sheet and we give you an example in this section.

EFFECTIVE COMMUNICATION

At a recent trade show in biotechnology many of the vendors, particularly those of start-up companies, gave no real understanding of what they did. Walking up to a booth at a trade show is like putting together a good elevator pitch, which we discussed earlier. Much like an entrepreneur seeking capital, exhibiting at a trade show needing to think of it as a passive elevator pitch; how does walk-by audience respond? Most new ventures do not have concise pitches, physical or verbal. They use lots of words, but what is being done is never clearly explained. On rare occasions one finds a new venture with a pitch that is interesting and encourages one to learn more. Good elevator pitches, booths, printed marketing materials, and business plans share the following three characteristics discussed below. First of all, a focused definition of the benefits of the products and/or services is always offered. Nobody really cares about how good a "thing" is; rather the primary concern appears to be what the benefits are to the entrepreneur. Second, new ventures, particularly those offering new products or new ways of doing things, often cannot explain what is done since the focus is entirely on details of how things are done. Rather than describing these details, one should start by mentioning a well-known company that the individual knows. Then explain the positive differences between the well-known company and the new venture. This allows other persons to grasp what the firm does, the benefits offered, and the advantages over competition. This means, obviously, that one does the necessary homework about the competition and what is important to potential customers or investors. The third thing we suggest in any elevator pitch is how to fulfill an unmet need. That unmet need may be the result of competitors not providing an adequate product or service to customers or new needs, wants, and fears. One should stress how they differ from competitors and how this allows the new venture to meet these needs, wants, and fears.

Remember to be careful when comparing with others since rarely are all competitors bad. Perfecting the elevator pitch can have a significant impact on the success of a new venture and a poor one can be the "kiss of death." As a final word, any elevator pitch to a potential investor should provide evidence of what the investor will get from the investment in terms of rate of return and the timing of the return.

THE WRITTEN BUSINESS PLAN

In prior chapters of this book we have tried to walk the reader through issues that all entrepreneurs need to address concerning their venture. Now is the time to take the answers to the checklist at the end of each chapter that I asked you to respond to and bring them together into a written plan. When writing a business plan the minimum sections you will need to have are

1. Executive Summary
2. Business/Concept Description
3. Market Analysis and Plan
4. Competition/Industry Analysis
5. Management Team
6. Operations Plan
7. Critical Risks (can be integrated throughout other sections)
8. Financial Plan and Assumptions

The above should be approximately twenty-five pages (not including financial spreadsheets or appendixes). It seems short but plans that are hundreds of pages do not get read, and frankly it is the executive summary that most people will read. If they have to plod through a tome to find out critical information, they will not read it. Over the years we have learned from hundreds of plans that people fatigue if they have to read more than twenty-five to thirty pages, and frankly entrepreneurs need to learn to be focused and clear in what they write and present. Our rule for visual presentations is no more than fifteen slides at maximum. We also believe that you should limit appendixes to fifteen pages. Your whole business plan should not exceed forty pages. Keep the font size big enough so that people do not go blind reading it (likewise for the spreadsheet numbers). If people want to see more detail on a given area, then have a longer version of each subsection, especially marketing and operational plans. Appendixes should be provided as necessary. The most common and essential appendixes are management resumes, product materials, and tax returns (if an existing business). When assembling a plan be sure to put it in the proper order (consistent with the order of topics in the executive summary). Be sure to include a cover page (with firm logo and name) and a "Table of Contents" with page numbers. The final product should be bound, preferably with a binding that allows the reader to turn and photocopy the pages easily.

CAUTIONS AND RED FLAGS

Every presentation, booth, and written plan creates red flags to viewers and readers. Some are words or phrases the entrepreneur uses to describe the firm.

Among the more obvious fluff phrases are "world class," "state-of-the-art," "everyone wants our product/service," and "a new and exciting opportunity." The real issue is to show that the venture is world class and state-of-the-art. This means the entrepreneur needs to show substance, not just acclaim these as virtues. Readers see red when they read statements like "we believe" and "word of mouth marketing" instead of giving specific data to understand how these will work. For those with college education we blanch when seeing excessive technology or industry jargon or excessive use of MBA jargon like SWOT, Porter's Five Forces, and the like. Every investor comments on hating to see "straight line projections for growth." Investors worry if they see "the CEO is not taking salary" or the infamous "according to our conservative cash flow projections." The reality is that most cash-flow projects are grossly optimistic. Other red flags include undefined acronyms (such as FIT, EBTDA, DNA, and RNA) in excess. The same acronyms have different meanings in different disciplines.

What are less obvious to the entrepreneur are things like market-size estimates in the billions, cash-flow projects that make the firm bigger than Microsoft and General Motors combined at the end of five years, and the delusion of "the firm breaks even in the first week of operations." This does not even happen even in dealing drugs. Another big issue that raises red flags is the critical management team's members missing. Who is running the venture is a major concern to anyone wanting to invest or join the firm. It is totally frustrating when there is no clear statement of the concept (or it appears on page 10 of the appendix). Finally there are issues of misspellings and poor grammar. If the entrepreneurs cannot check their work on the written plan, marketing materials, or presentation, then how can investors trust them to take care when operating the venture. A subtler red flag to investors is the response the entrepreneur has to a deal and term sheet. If the entrepreneurs act like they have never seen one of these and must talk to an attorney, the investor sees a "naïve entrepreneur." Remember that impression management is critical for the success of any entrepreneur. Credibility is like virginity, you lose it but once.

WRITING TIPS TO REMEMBER

When writing a business plan there are things some fundaments to remember. The first is brevity. It takes more effort to be brief than to ramble (another reason for limiting the length of business plans and presentations). An example of some poor writing is "Our activities in this area date back to the 1870s and we have built upon this one-hundred plus years experience to develop, without question, the most complete, accurate and selective mailing list products available anywhere in the world" (thirty-eight words). A better way to say the same thing is "Since 1870 we have built a world-wide reputation for lists that are selective, accurate, and thorough" (sixteen words).

Too many plans would put a reader to sleep. Remember in a business plan the entrepreneur is telling a story, so expressiveness is important. Open with a sentence that grabs attention. An example of a poor way to open a paragraph is "Most business owners are so busy handling everything from accounting to advertising that they don't take the time to set goals, measure results, and plan the long term success of their business" (thirty-two words). A better way that also reduces words is "What gets measured, gets done and experience proves that if you can't measure results someday there may not be any" (twenty-five words). Begin with something strong and have powerful endings, as this is what readers remember.

Memorable sentences plant the essential thoughts in the reader's mind using compelling syntax and cadence. An example of a poor ending is "Following six years of below average rainfall in the Napa Valley, the 1993 season produced abundant rain throughout winter and spring, creating optimal soil moisture to ensure full maturation of the fruit throughout the growing cycle and harvest" (thirty-eight words). Save words and make a stronger impact with "After six dry years, Napa Valley had weather that produced ripe, perfect fruit in 1993" (fifteen words).

Finally, there is the reality that English is the international business language and requires correct word usage, especially from native speakers. Please use words correctly. It will produce a much stronger image through writing and speech. For example, there is incorrect use of the word "anxious" (expecting stress and agitation) when what is meant is "eager" (expecting pleasure and comfort). To paraphrase Thomas Paine, "these are the plans that try investors' patience."

CONFIDENTIALITY AGREEMENTS

While confidentiality agreements normally are a part of the legal environment we include a discussion of these here as an entrepreneur will either be asked to sign a confidentiality agreement or nondisclosure agreement (NDA) or will need to consider having someone sign one. While in principle the idea of confidentiality is important, it is important to remember to never expect such a document to protect you from those who you would not trust to keep anything confidential. Never normally divulge detailed technical or actual financial information without one, especially to outsiders. However, if asking someone for advice on a plan as it is being developed, do not "insult them" by asking them to sign a nondisclosure. They may well hand back an invoice for services rendered. We do suggest that entrepreneurs ask potential early stage employees to sign NDAs if sharing proprietary information with them.

However, it is important to note that most venture capitalists and many angel investors will not sign an NDA given the number of business plans they see often covering the same fundamental concept or technology. They are in the business of keeping confidences, and entrepreneurs are usually safe to hand a business plan to venture capitalists without a confidentiality statement. It is always helpful to check out anyone prior to giving them any plan or proprietary information. A little due diligence goes a long way. If investors are really interested in detailed information, then they might sign one if progressing to the predeal term-sheet phase. When putting together an NDA you can certainly use a lawyer, but make sure you keep in mind the following:

1. Participants agree that data (including financial data) disclosed in written form will be clearly marked as confidential, and that all ideas, comments, and opinions contained within those plans will remain confidential.

2. Participants agree that information disclosed in oral form will be considered confidential.

3. Participants agree not to disclose any data, ideas, or plans to any third party without express written permission of the participants from whom such data came, except that participants will not be prevented from using or disclosing information

   a. which participants can demonstrate, by written record, was previously known to them;

   b. which is now, or becomes in the future, public knowledge other than through acts by a member participant;

   c. which is lawfully obtained by a participant from sources independent of this project.

DEAL AND TERM SHEETS

One of the areas in which many new entrepreneurs have problems is when they get their first deal and term sheet. Here it is important to understand what to look for in such a document and bring in a lawyer only after reviewing the document from a strategic business standpoint. The entrepreneur needs to know if the deal is consistent with the businesses' needs. If a lawyer does it, from a legal standpoint it might be fine, but from an entrepreneurial one, it might not. Also, any good investor is going to expect the entrepreneurs to understand the fundamentals of such sheets. If they do not, this is another red flag.

DEAL SHEET EXERCISE

Below is a deal and term sheet which should be read and which will then be followed by questions.

Memorandum of Terms for Private Placement of Equity Securities

In (1) Funk-alicious Technology Inc. and related entities ("FTI") and (2) entities related to the present and future development of Flux Capacitor technologies or derivations thereof (the "Capacitor Business"). Collectively, each of these entities is hereinafter referred to as the "Company."

Introduction. This Term Sheet is not intended to be, or to evidence, any legally binding agreement or commitment, except as set forth below in the sections entitled Publicity, Access to Information, and Exclusivity.

Proposed Private Placement. The Company and Investors propose a private placement of shares of Series B Convertible Preferred Stock (the "Series B Stock") and Preferred Stock Warrants (the "Warrants") (collectively the "Equity Securities") on the following terms:

Aggregate Amount:	$7,000,000 – Series B Stock $500,000 – Warrants $7,500,000 – Total
Investor *Commitments:* Series B Stock:	$3,000,000 – Venture Capital Partners ("VCP") $1,000,000 – Secondary Partners (the "Secondary Group") $3,000,000 – [Other Investor(s)]
Warrant:	$214,285 – Venture Capital Partners $71,430 – Secondary Partners $214,285 – [Other Investor(s)]
Relevant Terms of Series *B Stock:* Per Share Price and Capitalization:	22,500 shares at $311.11 per share, assuming current fully diluted shares outstanding of 90,000. Based on a full subscription, the Series B Stock will represent ownership equal to an aggregate of 20% of FTI's equity on a fully diluted basis (note: percentage reflects a total enterprise valuation of $35 million).
Dividends:	4% per annum in cash or in-kind, cumulative and *pari passu* to the existing Series A Preferred Stock.
Conversion:	Each share of Series B Stock is convertible at the option of the holder at anytime initially into one (1) share

of Common Stock. The conversion ratio is subject to adjustment for stock splits, stock dividends, and consolidations and to antidilution provisions discussed below. The Series B Stock is subject to automatic conversion upon the effective date of an underwritten public offering of Common Stock for account of the Company with net proceeds of not less than $20 million.

Price Protection / "Full Ratchet":

At any time prior to conversion or redemption, if the Company issues equity or equity-related securities, at an effective price per share less than that paid by the Investors, then the effective conversion price for the Series B Stock shall be adjusted downward to reflect such lower price, subject to a "pay-to-play" provision.

Redemption:

The earlier of an Initial Public Offering with gross proceeds to the Company of not less than $20 million or Five (5) years from the date of issuance. Upon redemption, the holders of the Series B Stock will be entitled to receive their per share purchase price, plus any declared but unpaid dividends.

Liquidation Preference:

In the event of any liquidation, dissolution, or winding up of the Company, the holders of the Series B Stock will be entitled to receive their per share purchase price, plus any accrued and unpaid dividends ("liquidation preference") before any payment is made to the holders of Common Stock; thereafter the Series B stockholders, Series A stockholders and the Common stockholders will participate in the distribution of proceeds on an "as-converted" basis.

Matters Requiring Class Voting:

A consolidation, merger, or share exchange of the Company where shareholders of the Company do not continue to hold at least 50.1% interest in the successor entity, or a sale of all or substantially all of the Company's assets, shall require the consent of a super majority of the holders of the Series B Stock or shall be deemed to be a liquidation or winding up for purposes of the Liquidation Preference.

Other Features:

Pari passu to the existing Series A Preferred Stock.

Relevant Terms of
Preferred Stock
Warrants:
  Exercise Price:

The Investors shall receive a Warrant to purchase their pro rata, fully diluted equity interest in the Capacitor Business. Based on a full subscription, such right shall represent an ownership interest equal to 20%. The effective exercise price of the Warrant is subject to various mutually agreed upon milestones which will be scheduled in the definitive documents. One such milestone will be the completion of and delivery of a fully functional prototype by July 31, 1999. Assuming full completion of the milestones by July 31, 1999, the Warrant shall be exercisable for Convertible Preferred Stock with a purchase price of $13 million, representing an enterprise value of $65 million. Thereafter, the enterprise value shall decrease by $3 million per month for ten months. However, in no case shall the enterprise value be less than $35 million. For months 19 on, the following formula will apply:

Where:
Target Enterprise Value ("TEV") = $65 million
Price Reduction ("PR") = $3 million
Time ("T") = Number of Months beyond 7/31/99
$$(TEV-PR(T))*.2$$

Warrant Expiration:

The earlier of (1) 30 days following the completion and delivery of a fully functional prototype; (2) ten (10) years from the date of issuance; or (3) the effective date of an underwritten public offering of Common Stock for account of the Company with net proceeds of not less than $20 million.

Matters Requiring
Class Voting:

A consolidation, merger or share exchange of the Capacitor Business where shareholders of the Company do not continue to hold at least 50.1% interest in the successor entity, or a sale of all or substantially all of the Company's assets, shall require the consent of a majority of the holders of the Warrants. Additionally, any issuance of stock, debt financing, or other financing sources shall require the consent of a majority of the holders of the Warrants.

Use of Proceeds:	The Series B Stock proceeds shall be used for (1) the completion of a commercially viable *Flux-o-rama*™ product (2) the building of the corporate infrastructure and (3) working capital requirements of the Company, as defined by a mutually agreed upon operating plan.

The Warrant proceeds shall be used to fund the initial development of the Capacitor Business, as defined by a mutually agreed upon operating plan. |
Employee Stock:	No additional shares of Common Stock or Incentive Stock Options are contemplated being issued as part of this transaction. Future increases in Common Stock for option grants will be at the sole discretion of the Board of Directors based upon the recommendation of a compensation committee.
Board of Directors:	The Company's Board of Directors will consist of seven (7) members. The Series B and Series A preferred stockholders shall have the right to appoint three (3) members, consisting of one VCP designee, one Secondary Group designee and one [Other Investor] designee. Each institutional investor shall also have board visitation rights. FTI shall have the right to appoint three (3) such members, including a management representative. The seventh seat shall be held by an outside director that is mutually acceptable to all of the above parties. The out-of-pocket expenses incurred by the representatives of the Investors in relation to attendance at board meetings will be borne by the Company. At Closing, the Board shall form audit and compensation committees, each of which shall be comprised of three (3) members. The Investors' designees shall comprise one (1) of three (3) such members.
Exclusivity:	Upon acceptance of this term sheet and until the earliest to occur of February 28, 1998, or the mutually written agreed abandonment of the proposed transaction, the Company agrees not to discuss potential financings, mergers or acquisitions without the prior consent of the Investors.
Target Closing Dates:	The target Initial Closing for VCP and the Company is January 15, 1998. Other Investors, including the

Secondary Group, shall have 120 days from the completion of the Initial Closing to invest on the same terms as VCP.

Publicity:

No press release notice, disclosure or any other publicity concerning the proposed transaction shall be issued, given, or disseminated by either party without the approval of the other party.

Access to Information:

Pending execution of a purchase agreement ("Purchase Agreement"), the Company shall provide the Investors complete access to all contracts, financial statements, records, and other material necessary to complete their due diligence. The Investors agree to maintain the confidentiality of such materials.

Fees and Expenses:

The Company will pay at the Closing (1) the reasonable legal and consulting/advisory fees of the Investors related to the transaction (2) the reimbursement of out-of-pocket expenses not to exceed $15,000; (3) VCP's Small Business Association processing fee (2% of VCP's investment); and (iv) the reimbursement of on-going out-of-pocket expenses incurred by the Secondary Group.

Additionally, if VCP or its affiliates is instrumental in assisting the Company with any subsequent financing, a mutually agreed upon financing fee will be paid to VCP.

Investor's Counsel:

Beavis & Butt-head

Purchase Agreement:

The investment shall be made pursuant to a Purchase Agreement reasonably acceptable to the Investors and the Company. Such agreement shall contain in addition to the provisions herein, among other things: (1) various traditional provisions, including representations and warranties; (2) use of proceeds; (3) Employment Agreements with various Key Executives; (4) indemnifications; (5) registration rights; (6) antidilution provisions, first right of refusal, right of cosale, preemptive rights, and other protective provisions, (7) confirmation of the Company's status as a Small Business, as defined in the Small Business Investment Act; (8) certain affirmative and negative covenants.

Conditions to Initial
Closing:

The obligation of the Investors to consummate the proposed transaction will be subject to fulfillment of the following conditions:

1. Satisfactory completion by the Investors of their business and financial review of the Company.

2. Delivery of a satisfactory opinion by independent legal counsel to the Company regarding patents issued and pending.

3. In exchange for various Flux Capacitor technology licenses or other rights, FTI shall receive a 2.5% equity interest in the Capacitor Business.

4. The engagement of an executive search firm for the purposes of identifying CEO candidates to be hired no later than 6/30/98.

5. Management's delivery of a mutually acceptable operating and strategic plan. Such plan shall include only those technologies relating to or building upon Flux Capacitor technologies. The Company and its existing shareholders shall make appropriate Representations and Warranties regarding those technologies which they believe do not relate to or build upon the Company's technologies.

6. Satisfactory completion by the Investors of background checks on Key Executives.

7. Execution of definitive agreements satisfactory to legal counsel to the Investors and the Company.

8. Delivery of an opinion by independent legal counsel to the Company satisfactory to legal counsel to the Investors.

Nature of Term Sheet:

This term sheet is not legally binding and is subject to completion of due diligence provided, however, that the provisions designated "Publicity" and "Access to Information" and "Exclusivity" shall be legally binding upon and enforceable against the Company. This term sheet (1) shall be governed by the laws of the State of California, (2) may not be amended or modified except by an instrument in writing signed by each of the parties hereto, and (3) may be executed in one or more counterparts.

Acknowledged and
Agreed to by:

Venture Capital Partners   Funkalicious Technologies Incorporated

_____   _____

Name: Daddy Big-bucks   Name:

Title: Partner   Title:

Secondary Partners

_____

Name: Money Bags

Title: Partner

DEAL SHEET QUESTIONS AND OBSERVATIONS

FIRST-ROUND QUESTIONS

1. What is the overall flavor of the deal structure?
2. What are the risks that are being addressed in the term sheet?
3. What is the most critical item of this deal?
4. Would you do a "pari passu" deal?

FIRST OBSERVATIONS

This is a syndication of deal and it is a second-round financing. There is no preference of first- over second-round financing. Investors end up with 20 percent of company, but there is a "baiting" the company with an evaluation. One should note that "pari passu" means "at the same rate."

SECOND-ROUND QUESTIONS

1. What is the valuation(s) of the firm?
2. What role does the "ratchet" term do to the firm?
3. What about the board of directors?

Second Observations

One can come up with a range of $35 million to $65 million in $3 million lots, depending on the delivery of prototype. The "ratchet" protects second investors by saying they can play at any new price. It is important to note that each round of financing does not occur in a vacuum. One should also note that the firm will have seven directors: three chosen by investors, three chosen by the company, and one jointly chosen to serve as a tiebreaker.

Third-round Questions

1. What are the costs of doing this deal?
2. What about the voting preference for series B?
3. If things go badly, how much of the firm does the VC own?
4. Why is the VC's percentage so low?
5. What are the conditions of the deal?
6. What is the protection for prior investors?

Third-round Observations

The first thing one should have noted is that the deal requires covering VC's costs such as legal fees, out-of-pocket, consulting fees, and that there is a financing fee (most likely the Lehman formula with a decreasing percentage of the deal based on the amount being funded). For those that worry about losing some "percentage" of ownership, the percentage really does not change as the warrants are "soft" and do not really add much to VC's share. One should have also noted that there are some fairly standard employment agreements, but note the demand to hire a new CEO. This says they have a concern about management and want to put the team leader on notice. Another way to come to this conclusion is to see that they have made the demand concerning the development of a strategic plan mutually acceptable to investors. One should have also noted that prior investors have 120 days to invest at the new terms.

PUTTING A PLAN TOGETHER: THE STAND-ALONE SUMMARY

The following is a stand-alone executive summary of a business plan constructed by a team of MBA students, under one of the author's direction, at Florida International University. This plan was never executed. We include this here to give you an example of a typical stand-alone executive summary and to help the reader learn what should go into such a document as well as to give the reader the chance to practice the skills we have discussed throughout this book. We suggest reading this summary and then trying to identify the kinds of issues addressed in earlier chapters.

Ciao! Foods Executive Summary

Making cooking dinner at home a simpler, healthier, and more enjoyable experience for busy professionals throughout the United States.

Important Notice

The following document is presented for informational purposes only. It is not intended to be, and is not, a prospectus, offering memorandum or private placement memorandum. The information in this business plan may not be complete and may be changed, modified or amended at any time by the company, and is not intended to, and does not, constitute representations and warranties of the company.

The company has only recently been formed under the original name "Castle Street Foods, Inc.," is a "start up operation" and has not had any operating history on which to base an evaluation of its business and prospects. Therefore, the information contained herein is inherently speculative.

The information in this business plan is also inherently forward-looking information. Among other things, the information discusses the company's future expectations, contains projections of the company's future results of operations or its financial condition, or states other "forward looking" information. There may be events in the future that the company cannot accurately predict or are over which the company can control, and the occurrence of such events may cause the company's actual results to differ materially from the expectations described herein.

This business plan constitutes confidential and proprietary information and may not be copied, faxed, reproduced or otherwise distributed by you, and the contents of this business plan may not be disclosed by you, without the company's express written consent.

1.0 EXECUTIVE SUMMARY

For millions of busy American professionals, the question that plagues them all toward the end of every workday is:

"What am I going to eat for dinner tonight?"

Although the options are endless by making a stop at the grocery or a local restaurant, they leave much to be desired. By 5:30 PM, grocery-store lines are usually long and grocery-store parking lots are full. Take-out and delivery options, while convenient, average 300–400 more calories and 20–25 grams of fat more than the suggested serving size by the USDA. The result of this phenomenon is a growing need for a marriage between health and convenience.

Ciao! Foods has been formed to answer this need with a revolutionary concept we call "*Ciao!* Bags" that puts a new twist on the ready-made dinner. *Ciao!* Bags are dinner kits that provide our customers with all of the food ingredients they need to prepare a healthy meal at home that any professional chef would envy. To add to the *Ciao!* Bag's convenience, all of our meals can be prepared in ten minutes or less.

However, the conveniences of our *Ciao!* Bags do not end with the packaging. Not only can our customers pick up at least ten different ingredients needed for a full-course meal in one fell swoop; they can pick up these items on their way out of their office building! Our distribution system enables us to deliver fresh *Ciao!* Bags every day to many different convenient locations just in time for rush hour.

1.1 THE PRODUCT

Our *Ciao!* Bags will contain fresh individually packaged ingredients. A representation of what meal kits may look like can be seen in here. The packing pictured here is an insulated bag that will keep contents cool for up to three hours, designed to allow for the customers' commute time from the office to the home.

Meal preparation is user friendly and simple due to the *Ciao!* Bags' measured, chopped, and sliced ingredients. Ingredients are all measured to the serving size and some examples of what may be included are chopped garlic, exotic spices, or cooking sherry. Meals can be prepared easily even by those with little or no cooking ability in about ten minutes. It is anticipated that a single-sized *Ciao!* Bag will sell for $6.99–$8.99 and a two-person-sized *Ciao!* Bag will sell for $12.99–$15.99.

Ciao! Foods anticipates that during the first few months of operation 3 different meals will be offered each week. As systems and processes become more refined, *Ciao!* Foods will begin to offer between five and six different dinners each week. Some will be "old favorites" and others will be new. Consumers can find out what selections are available via Monday morning e-mails, Web site, and printed menus at distribution locations.

A representation of what a weekly printed menu may look like can be seen here.

Other dinner recipes may include:

- Mushroom Risotto with Portobello mushrooms.
- Sesame Salmon in soy sauce with vegetables.
- Fragrant Thai Chicken with Coconut and Rice
- Pan Fried Chicken & Pappardelle Pasta—topped with Pine Nuts.

1.2 The Core Business and Distribution

Initially, *Ciao!* Foods will target all of their marketing and sales efforts toward a segment of the marketplace based on geographical and demographical variables. *Ciao!* Foods will focus the majority of its efforts on the distribution and marketing of *Ciao!* Bags and outsource the menu design, ingredient sourcing, and meal production to a qualified third party supplier.

Ciao! Foods will target busy, working professionals employed at major office towers located in Atlanta, Georgia. With one of the nations' highest income growth rate at 3.8% and with CEO of *Ciao!* Foods, Michael Johnson's experience working and living there for six years, Atlanta, Georgia has been selected as the launch market.

To meet consumer's needs for convenience, *Ciao!* Foods plans to sell *Ciao!* Bags through two different types of distribution channels where target consumers already spend time before parking their car at home each night. Consumers can pick up their *Ciao!* Bags meal kits at manned kiosk locations inside their office buildings or they can purchase a *Ciao!* Bag from our refrigerated displays at various athletic clubs in Atlanta. It is anticipated that primary locations in year one will be at two large office towers where between 1,500 and 7,000 professionals work each day and at least 9 athletic clubs throughout Atlanta.

1.3 MEAL PRODUCTION AND DISTRIBUTION

Ciao! Foods is currently in negotiations with several internationally recognized third-party food suppliers that will design, source, and package the meals for sale the same day. The company further expects that any unsold meals will have an additional shelf life of one to two days. It is planned that manned kiosks will be open from mid-afternoon to approximately 9 PM evening depending on location. Athletic club locations will follow local retailer business hours.

1.4 MANAGEMENT

Ciao! Foods will be managed part-time by CEO—Tim Smith, Business Director—Mary Martin, and a Business Support Analyst—yet to be assigned. Additional full- and part-time staff will be contracted as needed and when kiosk sales points are opened. Specialist consultants will be contracted as needed.

1.5 FINANCING REQUIRED

The owner is requesting $650,000 for estimated first year Capital Expenditures that are required in order to establish the business operations. An estimated additional $170,000 in Working Capital is also required. Capital Expenditures and Working Capital amounts of $820,000 will cover the first 12 months of operation. This could increase based on final payment terms from key suppliers. It is anticipated that an additional $250,000 in capital expenditure will be needed to fund year two increases in distribution and promotion.

EXECUTIVE SUMMARY EXERCISE

The readers should now sit down and revise this executive summary to make it better based on what has been previously discussed in this volume. Practice on this executive summary before starting on your own. Do not be surprised if the process takes several versions. We have learned that the best executive summaries go through as many as thirty versions. This is where word craft and focus will pay great dividends.

Glossary

Accounts payable. The money the firm owes its suppliers for goods and services delivered on credit.

Accounts receivable. The money owed to the firm by customers who have bought goods and services on credit.

Angel investor. Wealthy individual who invests in private companies. These are sometimes found in formal groups headed by an archangel. Most major cities have these groups.

Audited financial statements. A firm's financial statement prepared and certified by a public accounting firm. You will need these if you are selling a business.

Balance sheet. Summary statement of a firm's financial position at a given time. It summarizes assets, liabilities, stock, and retained earnings. Please remember that a balance sheet balances, hence its name.

Book value. The common stock equity shown on the balance sheet minus liabilities and any preferred stock.

Break-even point. Typically, the sales volume at which a firm's net sales revenue equals its cost. This is one of the most important things every entrepreneur should know not only on the financial statement, but also from a strategic marketing/selling standpoint.

Cash flow. The difference between the firm's cash receipts and its cash payments in a given period. Entrepreneurs live and die on cash flow.

Common stock. Shares of ownership, or equity, in a corporation. In an LLC this will be membership percentage.

Cost of goods sold. The direct cost of a product or service. This should include not only material cost but also the labor to manufacture. Without this you cannot determine profit margin or even pricing.

Debt service. Payment of principal and interest required to cover borrowing in a given period. This might well vary if borrowing has been with credit cards.

Discounted cash flow. This is a method of evaluating by adjusting the cash flows for the time value of money. If an investor is going to put money in now expecting future cash flows, they will then discount those future cash flows back to their present value. The discount rate is whatever rate of return the investor expects.

Due diligence. This is the process of checking out both investors and individual entrepreneurs as to their potential and character. This also includes testing business plan assumptions as well as verification of factual material provided by an entrepreneur or investor.

First-round financing. This is first investment made by external investors. This is when you will first see a deal and term sheet.

Franchising. This is an organization in which the franchisor with a tested product or service package enters into a contractual relationship with franchisees to operate a firm using that product or service.

Future value. The value at a future date of a present amount of money. *See also* Discounted cash flow.

Goodwill. This is the difference between the purchase price of a company and the net value of its assets when purchased. Worry if this figure gets too big as it may say you are paying too much for the asset.

Gross margin. This is the gross profit as a percentage of net sales revenue. Once again you need to know the cost of goods sold to achieve this number.

Harvest. This is the realization of the value of an investment that can come from a sale or exiting the firm in some fashion such as an IPO.

Income statement. This is the summary of a firm's revenues, expenses, and profits over a specified time. *See also* Pro forma statements.

Initial Public Offering (IPO). A process by which a firm raises money and is listed on a stock exchange.

Limited Liability Company. A firm owned by "members" who either manage the firm or hire a manager. Members have the advantage of limited liability and are taxed like a subchapter S corporation without having to conform to the restrictions on that form.

Line of credit. An arrangement with a bank or vendor that states what you can buy on credit.

Net income. The income a firm has after all expenses and taxes have been paid. Sometimes known as the bottom line.

Net present value. This is the present value of future net cash flows minus the investment. If the net present value is greater than 0, then it may be an investment opportunity.

Partnership. A legal form of a business with one or more persons as coowners sharing profits, losses, and liability (unless a limited partner).

Pro forma statements. These are projected financial statements (as against actual statements) and include profit and loss, cash flows, and balance sheets.

Rate of return. The annual return on an investment. For example, if the original investment was $1000 and at the end of a year it was paid back as $1160, we would say the rate of return was 16 percent. This would not be a venture capitalist rate of return, but beats the current interest rate on a savings account.

Sole proprietorship. A form of business with one owner who is responsible for all the firm's liabilities. Most small businesses have this form.

Subchapter S corporation. A form of corporation in which the owners personally pay the corporation's income taxes. Obviously requires that profits flow from the firm to the individual shareholders.

Sweat equity. This is the equity the entrepreneurial team acquires based on work which has a future value because of those efforts. Entrepreneurs overvalue this, and investors typically undervalue this.

Term sheet. This is a summary of the conditions for a proposed investment either by an angel or by a venture capitalist.

Valuation. The market value of a firm. There are multiple ways to determine this.

Venture capitalist. A financial group specializing in providing equity to firms with a limited track record but with the expectation of substantial growth.

Further Resources

There is a growing number of resources available to entrepreneurs to help them scan the external environment and deal with the day-to-day operations of their ventures. In addition to the specific references cited in each of the chapters there is a broad range of information for those interested in entrepreneurship in general. These include formal and informal groups, as well as print and web-based information sources. These informational resources are constantly changing and growing so any list will be dated and incomplete, however, below we have listed those that in 2006–2007 seem the most useful. Many of these are general information sources for those in business as well as more specialized sources for entrepreneurs. There are numerous on-line forums, newsgroups, mailing lists, "blogs," and dedicated web sites for those interested in entrepreneurship and family-owned and managed firms. There are also sources of information for idea generation and keeping up with trends and changes in technology. Some of the web sites are by subscription.

Organizationally, there are local chambers of commerce in most cities, many of whom are focused on smaller firms. In addition, there are over 250,000 trade and professional associations in the United States alone that can provide specific industry sector information for the entrepreneur. Also there are specific organizations dedicated to entrepreneurs, those who provide services to them, and those who study them within academia. We encourage entrepreneurs to join such groups and to use any and all of these groups as critical parts of their networks.

GENERAL WEB SOURCES

Ask Website, www.ask.com.
Google Website, www.google.com.

GENERAL INFORMATION SOURCES

Business Week Magazine, www.businessweek.com.
Entrepreneur Magazine, www.entrepreneur.com.
Family Business Magazine, www.familybusinessmagazine.com.
Financial Times, www.ft.com.
INC. Magazine, www.inc.com/magazine.
Library of Congress, www.loc.gov.
New York Times, www.times.com.
Wall Street Journal, www.wsj.com.

INTEREST WEB SOURCES FOR ENTREPRENEURS

http://corpgov.net.
http://trendchart.cordis.lu.
www.coolhunting.com.
www.research.fi.
www.signalsmag.com.

ORGANIZATIONAL RESOURCES FOR ENTREPRENEURS

Coleman-Fannie May Candies Foundation, www.colemanfoundation.org.
Enterprise Ireland, www.enterprise-ireland.com.
Ewing Marion Kauffman Foundation, www.emkf.org.
Family Business Network, www.fbn-i.org.
Family Firm Institute, www.ffi.org.
Finnish National Technology Agency, www.tekes.fi.
Lowe Foundation, www.lowe.org.
MIT Enterprise Forum, http://enterpriseforum.mit.edu.
National Association of Corporate Directors, www.nacdonline.org.
National Federation of Independent Business, www.nfib.com.
Organization for Economic Cooperation and Development, www.oecd.org.
Senior Corp of Retired Executives, www.score.org.
Small Business Advancement National Center, www.sbaer.uca.edu.
U.S. Department of State, International Information Programs, http://usinfo.state.gov.
U.S. Small Business Administration, www.sba.gov.

ACADEMIC ORGANIZATIONS

European Foundation for Management Development, www.efmd.org.
Global Entrepreneurship Monitoring Consortium, www.gemconsortium.org.
International Council for Small Business, www.icsb.org.
National Collegiate Inventors and Innovators, www.nciia.org.
U.S. Association for Small Business and Entrepreneurship, www.usasbe.org.

UNIVERSITY BASED PROGRAMS

Blank Center for Entrepreneurship at Babson College, http://www3.babson.edu/eship
Eugenio Pino and Family Global Entrepreneurship Center at Florida International University, www.entrepreneurship.fiu.edu.
Global Access Program at University of California, Los Angeles, www.oid.ucla.edu/webcast/UCTU/titles/Entrepreneur.html.
Rice University, Alliance for Technology Entrepreneurship, http://www.alliance.rice.edu
Stanford University Technology Ventures Program, http://stvp.stanford.edu/.
University of Southern California, Greif Center for Entrepreneurial Studies, www.marshall.usc.edu/web/Lloydgreif.

ACADEMIC JOURNAL SOURCES

Entrepreneurship and Regional Development, www.tandf.co.uk/journals/titles/08985626.asp.
Entrepreneurship Theory and Practice, www.blackwellpublishing.com/journal.asp?ref=1042-2587.
Family Business Review, www.blackwellpublishing.com/journal.asp?ref=0894-4865.
Journal of Business Venturing, www.elsevier.com/wps/find/journaldescription.cws_home/505723/description.
Journal of Small Business Management, ww.blackwellpublishing.com/journal.asp?ref=0047-2778.

Index

ABOUT THE AUTHORS

ALAN L. CARSRUD is Executive Director, Global Entrepreneurship Center, Professor of Industrial and Systems Engineering, and Clinical Professor of Management at Florida International University. Previously, he served on the faculty at the Anderson School, UCLA, and directed the graduate programs in entrepreneurship at the University of Texas, Austin, and the University of Southern California. He has taught at Pepperdine University, Nangang Technological University in Singapore, Anahuac University in Mexico City, and the Australian Graduate School of Management in Sydney. He was on the start-up team at People Express Airlines and Founding Director of CytoSignal, a biotech firm, and has served as Vice-President for the International Council for Small Business, on the Board of Directors of the Family Firm Institute, and as Founding Associate Editor of the journal, *Entrepreneurship and Regional Development*.

MALIN E. BRÄNNBACK is Professor of International Business at Åbo Akademi University, Department of Business Studies, and Docent at the Swedish School of Economics and Business Administration and the Turku School of Economics and Business Administration in Finland. She has held a variety of teaching and research positions in such fields as strategic management, international marketing, organizational processes, and pharmacy. She has served on the organizing committees of numerous international conferences and on the editorial board of the *Journal of Decision Systems*, and has published widely on entrepreneurship, strategic management, biotechnology, and other topics in articles, monographs, and conference presentations.